CONTENTS

INTRODUCTION

Cupcakes and muffins are more popular than ever, especially as they are so quick and easy to make. Perfectly packaged in individual paper cases, they appeal to both adults and children alike. We include a scrumptious selection of recipes to suit all tastes, so prepare to be amazed at the variety of delicious bakes on offer!

Classic everyday cupcakes include temptations such as Lemon Drizzle Cupcakes and Chocolate Butterfly Cupcakes. To show off your baking flair, special occasion cupcakes feature delights such as Cherry Sundae Cupcakes and Rose Petal Cupcakes. Finally, for some fun and funky flavours, recipes such as Limoncello Cupcakes and Chilli Chocolate Cupcakes are sure to hit the spot.

Marvellous muffins can be rustled up in next to no time and are ideal for breakfast, brunch or afternoon tea. We include delicious everyday muffins, such as Blueberry Muffins and Triple Chocolate Muffins, as well as more special creations, such as Pistachio & Lime Muffins and Strawberry & Cream Muffins.

There is fantastic fun to be had when baking cupcakes and muffins and you don't need a lot of expensive or specialist equipment. In fact, you will probably already have everything you need in your kitchen. If you are a regular baker, then it is worth investing in a good quality cupcake tin and standard muffin tin. Mini muffin tins can be used to make mini cupcakes or muffins, and standard muffin tins can also be used to create larger American-style cupcakes. A variety of cupcake tins (6- and 12-hole), standard muffin tins (6- and 12-hole) and mini muffin tins (12- and 24-hole) are readily available, including non-stick metal and silicone ones.

A wide range of paper cases in a mind-boggling array of dazzling colours and fun patterns, as well as different sizes, designs and shapes are readily available.

To add a tasty element of surprise, fillings such as jam, fresh fruit, squares of chocolate or mini baked cake shapes or brownies can be hidden inside cupcake batter before baking. Butterfly cakes are impressive, layered or marbled cupcakes add interest, and cupcake mixtures can be coloured before baking for extra pizzazz.

Cupcakes can be iced and decorated simply or in more flamboyant styles. Buttercream, cream cheese frosting, fondant icing, Royal or glacé icing, whipped cream and chocolate ganache are all suitable toppings. Chocolate curls, shavings or leaves, fondant icing or marzipan shapes, and edible writing icing provide perfect decorations. To jazz up cupcakes even more or add an extra bit of bling, choose from a wide range of edible decorations, including sparkling sugar sprinkles, dazzling edible glitter, small sweets and chocolates or decadent sugar flowers.

Stunning displays of decorated cupcakes can be created using tiered cupcake stands or a cupcake tree stand, to provide an impressive centrepiece for a special celebration that is sure to make heads turn.

For extra feel-good factor, decorated cupcakes make great gifts, either packaged in cellophane bags and tied with pretty ribbon or raffia, or arranged in attractive gift boxes.

Cupcakes and muffins are best eaten on the day they are made, though this is unlikely to be a dilemma, as they will soon be devoured! Muffins are best served freshly baked and warm from the oven. Undecorated cupcakes can be stored in an airtight container for 2–3 days, while decorated cupcakes will keep for 1–2 days in an airtight container, depending on the topping. Most muffins and plain or buttercream-iced cupcakes can be frozen for up to 1 month.

CLASSIC CUPCAKES

VANILLA FROSTED CUPCAKES

Makes: 12

Prep: 25 mins, plus cooling

Cook: 15–20 mins

Ingredients

115 g/4 oz butter, softened

115 g/4 oz golden caster sugar

2 eggs, lightly beaten

115 g/4 oz self-raising flour

1 tbsp milk

crystallized rose petals, to decorate

Frosting

175 g/6 oz butter, softened

2 tsp vanilla extract

2 tbsp milk

300 g/10½ oz icing sugar, sifted

Method

1 Preheat the oven to 180°C/350°F/Gas Mark 4. Line a 12-cup muffin tin with paper cases.

2 Place the butter and sugar in a bowl and beat together until light and fluffy. Gradually beat in the eggs. Sift in the flour and fold in gently using a metal spoon. Fold in the milk.

3 Spoon the mixture evenly into the paper cases. Bake in the preheated oven for 15–20 minutes, or until well risen, golden and firm to the touch. Transfer to a wire rack and leave to cool.

4 To make the frosting, put the butter, vanilla extract and milk in a large bowl. Using an electric hand-held mixer, beat the mixture until smooth. Gradually beat in the icing sugar and continue beating for 2–3 minutes, or until the frosting is very light and creamy.

5 Spoon the frosting into a large piping bag fitted with a large star nozzle and pipe swirls of the frosting onto the top of each cupcake. Decorate each cupcake with crystallized rose petals.

★ **Variation**

These pretty cupcakes can also be decorated with mulitcoloured sprinkles, dragées, icing flowers or edible petals.

CLASSIC CUPCAKES

CHOCOLATE BUTTERFLY CUPCAKES

Makes: 12

Prep: 30 mins, plus cooling

Cook: 20 mins

Ingredients

125 g/4½ oz soft margarine

125 g/4½ oz caster sugar

150 g/5½ oz self-raising flour

2 large eggs

2 tbsp cocoa powder

25 g/1 oz plain chocolate, melted

Frosting

100 g/3½ oz butter, softened

225 g/8 oz icing sugar, sifted, plus extra for dusting

grated rind of ½ lemon

1 tbsp lemon juice

Method

1 Preheat the oven to 180°C/350°F/Gas Mark 4. Line a 12-cup bun tin with paper cases.

2 Place the margarine, caster sugar, flour, eggs and cocoa powder in a large bowl and, using an electric hand-held mixer, beat until the mixture is just smooth. Beat in the melted chocolate.

3 Spoon the mixture evenly into the paper cases. Bake in the preheated oven for 15 minutes, or until well risen and firm to the touch. Transfer to a wire rack and leave to cool.

4 To make the frosting, place the butter in a large bowl and beat until fluffy. Gradually add in the icing sugar, lemon rind and lemon juice, beating well with each addition.

5 Cut the top off each cake, using a serrated knife. Cut each cake top in half. Spread the frosting over the cut surface of each cake and push the two pieces of cake top into the frosting to form wings. Dust with icing sugar.

RED VELVET CUPCAKES

Makes: 10

Prep: 20 mins,
plus cooling

Cook: 18–20 mins

Ingredients

150 g/5½ oz butter, softened

150 g/5½ oz caster sugar

3 eggs, lightly beaten

150 g/5½ oz self-raising flour

1 tbsp cocoa powder

1 tsp vanilla extract

¼ tsp red food colouring

Frosting

250 g/9 oz mascarpone cheese

175 g/6 oz icing sugar

1 tsp lemon juice

Method

1 Preheat the oven to 180°C/350°F/Gas Mark 4. Line a muffin tin with 10 paper cases.

2 Place the butter and sugar in a bowl and beat together until light and fluffy. Gradually beat in the eggs. Sift the flour and cocoa powder into the mixture and fold in gently. Stir in the vanilla extract and red food colouring.

3 Spoon the mixture evenly into the paper cases. Bake in the preheated oven for 18–20 minutes, or until well risen and firm to the touch. Transfer to a wire rack and leave to cool.

4 To make the frosting, beat the mascarpone cheese in a bowl until creamy. Add the icing sugar and lemon juice and beat until smooth. Spread or pipe swirls of the frosting on top of the cupcakes.

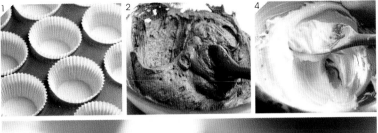

CHERRY & COCONUT CUPCAKES

Makes: 12

Prep: 25 mins, plus cooling

Cook: 20–25 mins

Ingredients

115 g/4 oz butter, softened

115 g/4 oz caster sugar

2 tbsp milk

2 eggs, lightly beaten

85 g/3 oz self-raising flour

½ tsp baking powder

85 g/3 oz desiccated coconut

115 g/4 oz glacé cherries, quartered

12 whole glacé, maraschino or fresh cherries, to decorate

Frosting

55 g/2 oz butter, softened

115 g/4 oz icing sugar

1 tbsp milk

Method

1 Preheat the oven to 180°C/350°F/Gas Mark 4. Line a 12-cup bun tin with paper cases.

2 Put the butter and sugar in a bowl and beat together until light and fluffy. Stir in the milk, then gradually add the eggs, beating well after each addition. Sift in the flour and baking powder and fold them in with the coconut. Gently fold in most of the quartered cherries.

3 Spoon the mixture evenly into the paper cases and scatter over the remaining quartered cherries. Bake in the preheated oven for 20–25 minutes, or until well risen, golden and firm to the touch. Transfer to a wire rack and leave to cool.

4 To make the frosting, put the butter in a bowl and beat until fluffy. Sift in the icing sugar and beat together until well mixed, gradually beating in the milk.

5 To decorate the cupcakes, use a piping bag fitted with a large star nozzle to pipe the frosting on top of each cupcake, then add a glacé, maraschino or fresh cherry to decorate.

COFFEE CUPCAKES

Makes: 10

Prep: 25 mins, plus cooling

Cook: 20–25 mins

Ingredients

175 g/6 oz butter, softened

175 g/6 oz soft light brown sugar

4 tsp instant espresso coffee powder

3 large eggs, lightly beaten

175 g/6 oz self-raising flour

1–2 tsp cocoa powder, to decorate

Frosting

140 g/5 oz full-fat soft cheese

70 g/2½ oz butter, softened

1 tsp vanilla extract

400 g/14 oz icing sugar, sifted

Method

1 Preheat the oven to 180°C/350°F/Gas Mark 4. Line a muffin tin with 10 paper cases.

2 Place the butter, sugar and coffee powder in a bowl and beat together until light and fluffy. Gradually add the eggs, a little at a time, beating well after each addition. Sift in the flour and fold in gently with a large metal spoon.

3 Spoon the mixture evenly into the paper cases. Bake in the preheated oven for 20–25 minutes, or until well risen and firm to the touch. Transfer to a wire rack and leave to cool.

4 To make the frosting, beat the cheese, butter and vanilla extract together until soft and creamy. Stir in half the sugar until smooth, then stir in the remainder. Beat well. Spoon or pipe a generous swirl of the frosting on top of each cupcake, then sift over a little cocoa powder.

DEVIL'S FOOD CHOCOLATE CUPCAKES

Makes: 18

Prep: 25 mins,
plus cooling & chilling

Cook: 25 mins

Ingredients

50 g/1¾ oz soft margarine

115 g/4 oz soft dark brown sugar

2 large eggs

115 g/4 oz plain flour

½ tsp bicarbonate of soda

25 g/1 oz cocoa powder

125 ml/4 fl oz soured cream

chocolate caraque, to decorate

Frosting

125 g/4½ oz plain chocolate, broken into pieces

2 tbsp caster sugar

150 ml/5 fl oz soured cream

Method

1 Preheat the oven to 180°C/350°F/Gas Mark 4. Line two bun tins with 18 paper cases.

2 Put the margarine, brown sugar, eggs, flour, bicarbonate of soda and cocoa powder in a large bowl and, using an electric hand-held mixer, beat together until just smooth. Using a metal spoon, fold in the soured cream.

3 Spoon the mixture evenly into the paper cases. Bake in the preheated oven for 20 minutes, or until well risen and firm to the touch. Transfer to a wire rack and leave to cool.

4 To make the frosting, put the chocolate into a heatproof bowl set over a saucepan of gently simmering water and heat until melted, stirring occasionally. Remove from the heat and allow to cool slightly, then whisk in the caster sugar and soured cream until combined. Spread the frosting over the tops of the cupcakes and leave to set in the refrigerator before serving. Serve decorated with chocolate caraque.

CLASSIC CUPCAKES

VANILLA BUTTERFLY CUPCAKES

Makes: 12

Prep: 30 mins,
plus cooling

Cook: 12–15 mins

Ingredients

140 g/5 oz butter, softened

140 g/5 oz golden caster sugar

½ tsp vanilla extract

2 large eggs, lightly beaten

140 g/5 oz self-raising flour

1–2 tbsp coloured sprinkles, to decorate

Frosting

85 g/3 oz butter, softened

175 g/6 oz icing sugar

1 tbsp orange juice

Method

1 Preheat the oven to 180°C/350°F/Gas Mark 4. Line a 12-cup bun tin with paper cases.

2 Place the butter, sugar and vanilla extract in a bowl and beat together until light and fluffy. Gradually add the eggs, a little at a time, beating well after each addition. Sift in the flour and fold in gently with a large metal spoon.

3 Spoon the mixture evenly into the paper cases. Bake in the preheated oven for 12–15 minutes, or until well risen, golden and firm to the touch. Transfer to a wire rack and leave to cool.

4 To make the frosting, beat together the butter, icing sugar and orange juice in a bowl until fluffy.

5 Cut the top off each cake, using a serrated knife. Cut each cake top in half. Spread the frosting over the cut surface of each cake and push two pieces of cake top into the frosting to form wings. Decorate with sprinkles.

CLASSIC CUPCAKES

PINEAPPLE CUPCAKES

Makes: 12

Prep: 25 mins,
plus cooling

Cook: 15–20 mins

Ingredients

115 g/4 oz butter, softened

115 g/4 oz caster sugar

2 eggs, lightly beaten

115 g/4 oz self-raising flour

3 canned pineapple rings, drained and finely chopped

Frosting

115 g/4 oz butter, softened

115 g/4 oz full-fat soft cheese

280 g/10 oz icing sugar, sifted

55 g/2 oz desiccated coconut

25 g/1 oz glacé pineapple, chopped, to decorate

Method

1 Preheat the oven to 180°C/350°F/Gas Mark 4. Line a 12-cup bun tin with paper cases.

2 Put the butter and caster sugar into a bowl and beat together until light and fluffy. Gradually beat in the eggs. Sift in the flour and fold in gently. Fold in the chopped pineapple.

3 Spoon the mixture evenly into the paper cases. Bake in the preheated oven for 15–20 minutes, or until well risen, golden and firm to the touch. Transfer to a wire rack and leave to cool.

4 To make the frosting, beat together the butter and soft cheese until smooth. Gradually beat in the icing sugar, then fold in the coconut.

5 Swirl the frosting over the tops of the cupcakes and decorate with the glacé pineapple.

WHITE CHOCOLATE & ROSE CUPCAKES

Makes: 12

Prep: 25 mins, plus cooling & chilling

Cook: 20–25 mins

Ingredients

115 g/4 oz butter, softened

115 g/4 oz caster sugar

1 tsp rose water

2 eggs, lightly beaten

115 g/4 oz self-raising flour

55 g/2 oz white chocolate, grated

sugar-frosted pink rose petals, to decorate

Frosting

115 g/4 oz white chocolate, broken into pieces

2 tbsp milk

175 g/6 oz full-fat soft cheese

25 g/1 oz icing sugar, sifted

Method

1 Preheat the oven to 180°C/350°F/Gas Mark 4. Line a 12-cup bun tin with paper cases.

2 Place the butter, sugar and rose water in a bowl and beat together until light and fluffy. Gradually beat in the eggs. Sift over the flour and fold in gently. Fold in the white chocolate.

3 Spoon the mixture evenly into the paper cases. Bake in the preheated oven for 15–20 minutes, or until well risen, golden and firm to the touch. Transfer to a wire rack and leave to cool.

4 To make the frosting, place the chocolate and milk in a heatproof bowl set over a saucepan of simmering water and heat until melted. Remove from the heat and stir until smooth. Cool for 30 minutes.

5 Put the soft cheese and icing sugar in a bowl and beat together until smooth and creamy. Fold in the chocolate. Chill in the refrigerator for 1 hour.

6 Swirl the frosting over the top of the cupcakes. Decorate with the sugar-frosted rose petals.

SALTED CARAMEL CUPCAKES

Makes: 12

Prep: 25 mins,
plus cooling

Cook: 30 mins

Ingredients

190 g/6¾ oz plain flour

1½ tsp baking powder

¼ tsp salt

115 g/4 oz butter, softened

100 g/3½ oz caster sugar

110 g/3¾ oz soft dark
brown sugar

1 tsp vanilla extract

1 tsp coffee extract

2 large eggs, lightly beaten

125 ml/4 fl oz milk

1 tsp sea salt flakes,
to decorate

Frosting

115 g/4 oz butter, softened

220 g/7¾ oz soft dark
brown sugar

90 ml/3 fl oz double cream

½ tsp salt

about 190 g/6¾ oz icing
sugar (see method)

Method

1 Preheat the oven to 180°C/350°F/Gas Mark 4.
Line a 12-cup bun tin with paper cases.

2 Sift together the flour, baking powder and
salt in a bowl. Put the butter, caster sugar and
brown sugar into a separate bowl and beat
until light and fluffy. Add the vanilla extract
and coffee extract, then add the eggs one
at a time, beating after each addition. Add half
of the flour mixture and the milk and beat until
incorporated. Add the remaining flour mixture
and fold in gently.

3 Spoon the mixture evenly into the paper cases.
Bake in the preheated oven for 20 minutes,
or until well risen, golden and firm to the touch.
Transfer to a wire rack and leave to cool.

4 To make the frosting, first prepare a caramel
sauce by melting the butter in a small saucepan
over a medium heat. Add the brown sugar,
cream and salt and cook, stirring constantly,
for about 4 minutes, or until the sugar is
completely dissolved. Remove from the heat
and set aside to cool.

5 Add the icing sugar to the caramel sauce and beat until the sugar is fully incorporated. Add more icing sugar, if necessary, to achieve a piping consistency. Spoon into a piping bag fitted with a star-shaped tip and pipe onto the cupcakes.

6 To decorate, sprinkle the cupcakes evenly with the sea salt flakes directly before serving.

GLUTEN-FREE RASPBERRY CUPCAKES

Makes: 12

Prep: 20 mins, plus cooling

Cook: 18–20 mins

Ingredients

2 eggs

175 g/6 oz caster sugar

1 tsp glycerine

150 g/5½ oz gluten-free self-raising flour

15 g/½ oz rice flour

½ tsp xanthan gum

1 tsp gluten-free baking powder

20 g/¾ oz ground almonds

35 g/1¼ oz gluten-free white chocolate drops

125 ml/4 fl oz sunflower oil

50 ml/2 fl oz milk

50 ml/2 fl oz single cream

½ tsp vanilla extract

24 fresh or frozen raspberries

Frosting (optional)

225 g/8 oz gluten-free icing sugar

60 g/2¼ oz butter, softened

70 g/2½ oz gluten-free soft cheese

1 tbsp milk or single cream

fresh raspberries, to decorate

Method

1 Preheat the oven to 180°C/350°F/Gas Mark 4. Line a 12-cup muffin tin with paper cases.

2 Whisk the eggs, sugar and glycerine in a large bowl until thick and fluffy. Sift the flours, xanthan gum, baking powder and ground almonds into a separate bowl.

3 Add the dry mixture to the wet mixture and fold in the chocolate drops. Add the oil, milk, cream and vanilla extract and whisk together to form a smooth mixture.

4 Spoon the mixture evenly into the paper cases then press two raspberries into the centre of each cupcake.

5 Bake in the preheated oven for 18–20 minutes, or until well risen, golden and firm to the touch. Transfer to a wire rack and leave to cool.

6 To make the frosting, whisk all the ingredients together in a large bowl until thick. Place in a piping bag and decorate each cupcake when completely cool.

CLASSIC CUPCAKES

SPICED APPLE CUPCAKES

Makes: 12

Prep: 25 mins, plus cooling

Cook: 30 mins

Ingredients

50 g/1¾ oz butter, softened

70 g/2½ oz demerara sugar

1 egg, lightly beaten

150 g/5½ oz plain flour

1½ tsp baking powder

½ tsp ground mixed spice

1 large cooking apple, finely chopped

1 tbsp orange juice

Topping

40 g/1½ oz plain flour

½ tsp ground mixed spice

25 g/1 oz butter

40 g/1½ oz caster sugar

Method

1 Preheat the oven to 180°C/350°F/Gas Mark 4. Line a 12-cup muffin tin with paper cases.

2 To make the topping, place the flour, mixed spice, butter and sugar in a large bowl and rub in with your fingertips until the mixture resembles fine breadcrumbs. Set aside.

3 Place the butter and sugar in a large bowl and beat together until light and fluffy, then gradually beat in the egg. Sift in the flour, baking powder and mixed spice and fold into the mixture, then fold in the chopped apple and orange juice.

4 Spoon the mixture evenly into the paper cases. Add the topping to cover the top of each cupcake and press down gently. Bake in the preheated oven for 30 minutes, or until well risen, golden and firm to the touch. Transfer to a wire rack to cool completely.

CLASSIC CUPCAKES

LEMON DRIZZLE CUPCAKES

Makes: 12

Prep: 20 mins, plus cooling

Cook: 20 mins

Ingredients

175 g/6 oz butter, softened

175 g/6 oz golden caster sugar

175 g/6 oz self-raising flour, sifted

1 tsp baking powder

3 large eggs

3 tbsp lemon curd

Topping

100 g/3½ oz granulated sugar

juice and grated rind 1 lemon

Method

1 Preheat the oven to 180°C/350°F/Gas Mark 4. Line a 12-cup bun tin with paper cases.

2 Put the butter, sugar, flour, baking powder and eggs in a large bowl and, using an electric hand-held mixer, beat until the mixture is just smooth. Fold in the lemon curd.

3 Spoon the mixture evenly into the paper cases. Bake in the preheated oven for 20 minutes, or until well risen, golden and firm to the touch. While the cupcakes are baking, mix the topping ingredients together in a bowl.

4 Remove the cupcakes from the oven and leave for 2 minutes, then spread some of the topping over each cupcake. Leave to cool in the tin – the topping will go crisp on cooling.

CLASSIC CUPCAKES

CHOCOLATE CHIP CUPCAKES

Makes: 18

Prep: 25 mins,
plus cooling & chilling

Cook: 25 mins

Ingredients

85 g/3 oz butter, softened

100 g/3½ oz caster sugar

2 eggs, lightly beaten

2 tbsp milk

55 g/2 oz plain chocolate chips

225 g/8 oz self-raising flour

25 g/1 oz cocoa powder, plus extra for dusting

Frosting

225 g/8 oz white chocolate, broken into pieces

150 g/5½ oz full-fat soft cheese

Method

1 Preheat the oven to 200°C/400°F/Gas Mark 6. Line two bun tins with 18 paper cases.

2 Beat together the butter and sugar until light and fluffy. Gradually add the eggs, beating well after each addition. Add a little of the flour if the mixture starts to curdle. Add the milk, then fold in the chocolate chips.

3 Sift together the flour and cocoa and fold into the mixture with a metal spoon.

4 Spoon the mixture evenly into the paper cases. Bake in the preheated oven for 20 minutes, or until well risen and firm to the touch. Transfer to a wire rack to cool.

5 To make the frosting, melt the chocolate in a heatproof bowl set over a saucepan of gently simmering water. Cool slightly. Beat the soft cheese until softened, then beat in the melted chocolate. Spread the frosting over each cake and leave to chill for 1 hour. Dust with a little cocoa before serving.

CLASSIC CUPCAKES

WHOLEMEAL APRICOT CUPCAKES

Makes: 14

Prep: 25 mins, plus cooling

Cook: 20–25 mins

Ingredients

115 g/4 oz butter, softened

85 g/3 oz light soft brown sugar

2 tbsp set honey

2 eggs, lightly beaten

115 g/4 oz plain wholemeal flour

1½ tsp baking powder

1 tsp ground mixed spice

85 g/3 oz ready-to-eat dried apricots, chopped

Topping

2 tbsp apricot jam, warmed and sieved

slices of ready-to-eat dried apricots, to decorate

Method

1 Preheat the oven to 190°C/375°F/Gas Mark 5. Line two bun tins with 14 paper cases.

2 Put the butter, sugar and honey in a bowl and beat together until light and fluffy. Gradually add the eggs, beating well after each addition. Sift in the flour, baking powder and mixed spice (tipping any bran left in the sieve into the bowl) and, using a metal spoon, fold them into the mixture with the chopped apricots.

3 Spoon the mixture evenly into the paper cases. Bake in the preheated oven for 15–20 minutes, or until well risen, golden and firm to the touch. Transfer to a wire rack to cool.

4 When the cupcakes are cool, brush the apricot jam over the top of the cupcakes and decorate each with a slice of apricot.

CLASSIC CUPCAKES

HUMMINGBIRD CUPCAKES

Makes: 24

Prep: 30 mins,
plus cooling

Cook: 20 mins

Ingredients

225 g/8 oz plain flour

1¼ tsp baking powder

¼ tsp bicarbonate of soda

2 ripe bananas

115 g/4 oz butter, softened

115 g/4 oz caster sugar

½ tsp vanilla extract

2 eggs, lightly beaten

4 tbsp soured cream

55 g/2 oz roughly chopped pecan nuts

25 g/1 oz whole pecan nuts, to decorate

Frosting

115 g/4 oz butter, softened

175 g/6 oz icing sugar

Method

1 Preheat the oven to 190°C/375°F/Gas Mark 5. Line two 12-cup bun tins with 24 paper cases.

2 Sift together the flour, baking powder and bicarbonate of soda. Peel the bananas, put them in a bowl and mash with a fork. Put the butter, sugar and vanilla in a bowl and beat together until light and fluffy. Gradually add the eggs, beating well after each addition. Stir in the mashed bananas and soured cream. Using a metal spoon, fold in the sifted flour mixture and chopped nuts.

3 Spoon the mixture evenly into the paper cases. Bake in the preheated oven for 20 minutes, or until well risen, golden and firm to the touch. Transfer to a wire rack and leave to cool.

4 To make the frosting, put the butter in a bowl and beat until fluffy. Sift in the icing sugar and mix together well. Spread the frosting on top of the cupcakes and decorate with the pecans before serving.

CHOCOLATE-CENTRED CUPCAKES

Makes: 9

Prep: 20 mins, plus cooling

Cook: 20 mins

Ingredients

175 g/6 oz soft margarine

175 g/6 oz caster sugar

3 large eggs

250 g/9 oz self-raising flour

3 tbsp cocoa powder

175 g/6 oz plain chocolate

icing sugar, for dusting

Method

1 Preheat the oven to 190°C/375°F/Gas Mark 5. Line a bun tin with 9 paper cases.

2 Put the margarine, caster sugar, eggs, flour and cocoa powder in a large bowl and, using an electric hand-held mixer, beat together until just smooth.

3 Spoon half of the mixture into the paper cases. Using a teaspoon, make an indentation in the centre of each cake. Break the chocolate evenly into 9 squares and place a piece on top of each indentation, then spoon the remaining cake mixture on top.

4 Bake in the preheated oven for 20 minutes, or until well risen and firm to the touch. Leave the cupcakes to cool for 2–3 minutes before serving warm, dusted with sifted icing sugar.

CHOCOLATE COOKIE CUPCAKES

Makes: 12

Prep: 35 mins, plus cooling

Cook: 33–35 mins

Ingredients

250 g/9 oz uncooked ready-made chocolate chip cookie dough

190 g/6¾ oz plain flour

1½ tsp baking powder

¼ tsp salt

115 g/4 oz butter, softened

50 g/1¾ oz caster sugar

100 g/3½ oz soft light brown sugar

2 tsp vanilla extract

2 large eggs, lightly beaten

125 ml/4 fl oz milk

50 g/1¾ oz plain chocolate chips, to decorate

Frosting

3 large egg whites

160 g/5¾ oz soft light brown sugar

160 g/5¾ oz butter, softened

1½ tsp vanilla extract

Method

1 Preheat the oven to 190°C/375°F/Gas Mark 5. Line a 12-cup bun tin with paper cases.

2 Drop rounded spoonfuls of cookie dough into the paper cases and bake in the preheated oven for 8–10 minutes, or until the cookies have started to brown. Remove from the oven and reduce the oven temperature to 180°C/350°F/Gas Mark 4.

3 Sift together the flour, baking powder and salt in a bowl. Put the butter, caster sugar and brown sugar into a separate bowl and beat until light and fluffy. Add the vanilla extract, then add the eggs gradually, beating after each addition. Add half of the flour mixture and the milk and beat until incorporated. Add the remaining flour mixture and mix.

4 Spoon the mixture evenly over the cookie bases in the paper cases. Bake in the preheated oven for 20 minutes, or until well risen, golden and firm to the touch. Transfer to a wire rack and leave to cool.

5 To make the frosting, put the egg whites and brown sugar in a heatproof bowl set over a saucepan of gently simmering water and whisk until the sugar is completely dissolved. Remove

from the heat and whisk the mixture for 4–5 minutes. Add the butter, 2 tablespoons at a time, and continue to beat until it holds stiff peaks. Add the vanilla extract and beat until just combined.

6 Spoon the frosting into a piping bag fitted with a star-shaped tip and pipe onto the cupcakes, then sprinkle with chocolate chips.

CRANBERRY CUPCAKES

Makes: 12

Prep: 15 mins,
plus cooling

Cook: 15–20 mins

Ingredients

75 g/2¾ oz butter, softened,
or soft margarine

100 g/3½ oz caster sugar

1 large egg, lightly beaten

2 tbsp milk

100 g/3½ oz self-raising flour

1 tsp baking powder

75 g/2¾ oz frozen
cranberries

Method

1 Preheat the oven to 180°C/350°F/Gas Mark 4.
Line a 12-cup bun tin with paper cases.

2 Place the butter and sugar in a large bowl and
beat together until light and fluffy, then gradually
beat in the egg and stir in the milk. Sift in the flour
and baking powder and fold into the mixture.
Gently fold in the frozen cranberries.

3 Spoon the mixture evenly into the paper cases.
Bake in the preheated oven for 15–20 minutes,
or until well risen, golden and firm to the touch.
Transfer to a wire rack and leave to cool.

PEANUT BUTTER CUPCAKES

Makes: 16

Prep: 25 mins, plus cooling

Cook: 25 mins

Ingredients

55 g/2 oz butter, softened

225 g/8 oz soft light brown sugar

115 g/4 oz crunchy peanut butter

2 eggs, lightly beaten

1 tsp vanilla extract

225 g/8 oz plain flour

2 tsp baking powder

100 ml/3½ fl oz milk

chopped unsalted peanuts, to decorate

Frosting

200 g/7 oz full-fat soft cheese

25 g/1 oz butter, softened

225 g/8 oz icing sugar

Method

1 Preheat the oven to 180°C/350°F/Gas Mark 4. Line two bun tins with 16 paper cases.

2 Put the butter, sugar and peanut butter in a bowl and beat together for 1–2 minutes, or until light and fluffy. Gradually add the eggs, beating well after each addition, then add the vanilla extract. Sift in the flour and baking powder and then, using a metal spoon, fold them into the mixture, alternating with the milk.

3 Spoon the mixture evenly into the paper cases. Bake in the preheated oven for 25 minutes, or until well risen, golden and firm to the touch. Transfer to a wire rack and leave to cool.

4 To make the frosting, put the soft cheese and butter in a bowl and beat together until smooth. Sift the icing sugar into the mixture and mix well. Put the frosting in a piping bag, fitted with a large star nozzle. When the cupcakes are cool, pipe a blob on top of each cupcake and decorate with the peanuts.

FROSTED BERRY CUPCAKES

Makes: 12

Prep: 40 mins, plus cooling

Cook: 15–20 mins

Ingredients

115 g/4 oz butter, softened, or soft margarine

115 g/4 oz caster sugar

2 tsp orange flower water

2 large eggs, lightly beaten

55 g/2 oz ground almonds

115 g/4 oz self-raising flour

2 tbsp milk

280 g/10 oz berries, fresh mint leaves, egg white and sugar, to decorate

Frosting

300 g/10½ oz mascarpone cheese

85 g/3 oz caster sugar

4 tbsp orange juice

Method

1 Preheat the oven to 180°C/350°F/Gas Mark 4. Line a 12-cup bun tin with paper cases.

2 Place the butter, caster sugar and orange flower water in a large bowl and beat together until light and fluffy. Gradually beat in the eggs. Stir in the ground almonds. Sift in the flour and, using a metal spoon, fold in gently with the milk.

3 Spoon the mixture evenly into the paper cases. Bake in the preheated oven for 15–20 minutes, or until well risen, golden and firm to the touch. Transfer to a wire rack and leave to cool.

4 To make the frosting, put the mascarpone, caster sugar and orange juice in a bowl and beat together until smooth.

5 Swirl the frosting over the top of the cupcakes. Brush the berries and mint leaves with egg white and roll in the sugar to coat. Decorate the cupcakes with the frosted berries and leaves.

CHOCOLATE PARADISE CUPCAKES

Makes: 16

Prep: 40 mins,
plus cooling & chilling

Cook: 33–35 mins

Ingredients

85 g/3 oz plain chocolate, broken into pieces

50 ml/2 fl oz milk

1 tbsp cocoa powder

115 g/4 oz butter, softened, or soft margarine

115 g/4 oz dark muscovado sugar

2 large eggs, lightly beaten

3 tbsp soured cream

175 g/6 oz plain flour

½ tsp bicarbonate of soda

Topping

115 g/4 oz white marshmallows

3 tbsp milk

300 ml/10 fl oz double cream

55 g/2 oz desiccated coconut

55 g/2 oz plain chocolate, melted

Method

1 Preheat the oven to 180°C/350°F/Gas Mark 4. Line two bun tins with 16 paper cases.

2 Place the chocolate, milk and cocoa powder in a heatproof bowl set over a saucepan of simmering water and leave until the chocolate has melted. Stir until smooth.

3 Place the butter and muscovado sugar in a large bowl and beat together until light and fluffy. Gradually beat in the eggs, then beat in the melted chocolate mixture and soured cream. Sift in the flour and bicarbonate of soda and, using a metal spoon, fold in gently.

4 Spoon the mixture evenly into the paper cases. Bake in the preheated oven for 18–20 minutes, or until risen and firm to the touch. Leave to cool.

5 Place the marshmallows and milk in a heatproof bowl set over a saucepan of simmering water. Leave until the marshmallows have melted, stirring occasionally. Leave to cool. Whip the cream until holding firm peaks, then fold into the marshmallow mixture with 35 g/1¼ oz of the desiccated coconut. Chill for 30 minutes.

6 Spread the topping over the cupcakes. Sprinkle over the remaining coconut. Spoon the melted chocolate into a piping bag and pipe criss-cross lines over the top of each cupcake. Leave to set.

CLASSIC CUPCAKES

LEMON POLENTA CUPCAKES

Makes: 14

Prep: 25 mins, plus cooling

Cook: 20 mins

Ingredients

115 g/4 oz butter, softened

115 g/4 oz golden caster sugar

finely grated rind and juice of ½ lemon

2 eggs, lightly beaten

55 g/2 oz plain flour

1 tsp baking powder

55 g/2 oz quick-cook polenta

crystallized violets, to decorate

Frosting

150 g/5½ oz mascarpone cheese

2 tsp finely grated lemon rind

25 g/1 oz icing sugar, sifted

Method

1 Preheat the oven to 180°C/350°F/Gas Mark 4. Line two bun tins with 14 paper cases.

2 Put the butter and sugar in a bowl and beat together until light and fluffy. Beat in the lemon rind and juice. Gradually beat in the eggs. Sift in the flour and baking powder and, using a metal spoon, fold gently into the mixture with the polenta.

3 Spoon the mixture evenly into the paper cases. Bake in the preheated oven for 20 minutes, or until well risen, golden and firm to the touch. Transfer to a wire rack and leave to cool.

4 To make the frosting, beat the mascarpone cheese until smooth then beat in the lemon rind and icing sugar. Spread the frosting over the cupcakes. Decorate each cupcake with a crystallized violet just before serving.

CLASSIC CUPCAKES

GLAZED MADEIRA CUPCAKES

Makes: 16

Prep: 25 mins,
plus cooling & setting

Cook: 20–25 mins

Ingredients

115 g/4 oz butter, softened

115 g/4 oz golden caster sugar

finely grated rind of ½ lemon

2 large eggs, lightly beaten

175 g/6 oz self-raising flour

40 g/1½ oz ground almonds

55 g/2 oz candied citron peel, thinly sliced

Topping

55 g/2 oz icing sugar

3 tsp warm water

Method

1 Preheat the oven to 180°C/350°F/Gas Mark 4. Line two bun tins with 16 paper cases.

2 Put the butter, sugar and lemon rind in a bowl and beat together until light and fluffy. Gradually beat in the eggs. Sift in the flour and, using a metal spoon, fold gently into the mixture with the ground almonds.

3 Spoon the mixture evenly into the paper cases. Put a slice of citron peel on the top of each cupcake. Bake in the preheated oven for 20–25 minutes, or until well risen. golden and firm to the touch. Transfer to a wire rack and leave to cool.

4 To make the topping, sift the icing sugar into a bowl and add enough warm water to make a runny glaze. Using a pastry brush, glaze the top of each cupcake with the topping. Leave to set.

CLASSIC CUPCAKES

NEAPOLITAN CUPCAKES

Makes: 12

Prep: 35 mins, plus cooling & chilling

Cook: 15–20 mins

Ingredients

140 g/5 oz self-raising flour

½ tsp baking powder

140 g/5 oz butter, softened, or soft margarine

140 g/5 oz caster sugar

2 large eggs

1 tsp vanilla extract

1 tbsp milk

1 tbsp cocoa powder mixed to a paste with 1½ tbsp hot water

chocolate strands, to decorate

6 ice-cream wafers, each cut into 4 triangles, to decorate

Frosting

175 g/6 oz full-fat soft cheese

115 g/4 oz butter, softened

350 g/12 oz icing sugar

1 tbsp strawberry jam, sieved

pink food colouring

Method

1 Preheat the oven to 180°C/350°F/Gas Mark 4. Line a 12-cup muffin tin with paper cases.

2 Sift the flour and baking powder into a large bowl. Add the butter, caster sugar and eggs and, using an electric hand-held mixer, beat together until just smooth.

3 Divide the mixture between two bowls. Beat the vanilla extract and milk into one of the bowls and the cocoa paste into the other bowl.

4 Place alternate teaspoonfuls of the mixtures into the paper cases. Bake in the preheated oven for 15–20 minutes, or until well risen and firm to the touch. Transfer to a wire rack and leave to cool.

5 To make the frosting, put the soft cheese and butter in a bowl and blend together with a spatula. Sift in the icing sugar and beat until smooth and creamy. Divide the mixture between two bowls and stir the jam and a little pink food colouring into one of the bowls. Cover and chill in the refrigerator for 30 minutes.

6 Place alternate spoonfuls of the frostings into a large piping bag fitted with a star nozzle. Pipe swirls of the frosting on the top of each cupcake. Sprinkle with chocolate strands and decorate each cupcake with two wafer triangles.

CLASSIC CUPCAKES

3

4

6

MOCHA CUPCAKES

Makes: 20

Prep: 25 mins, plus cooling

Cook: 25–30 mins

Ingredients

2 tbsp instant espresso coffee powder

85 g/3 oz butter, softened

85 g/3 oz caster sugar

1 tbsp clear honey

200 ml/7 fl oz water

225 g/8 oz plain flour

2 tbsp cocoa powder

1 tsp bicarbonate of soda

3 tbsp milk

1 large egg, lightly beaten

Topping

225 ml/8 fl oz whipping cream

cocoa powder, sifted, for dusting

Method

1 Preheat the oven to 180°C/350°F/Gas Mark 4. Line two bun tins with 20 paper cases.

2 Put the coffee powder, butter, sugar, honey and water in a saucepan and heat gently, stirring, until the sugar has dissolved. Bring to the boil, then reduce the heat and simmer for 5 minutes. Pour into a large heatproof bowl and leave to cool.

3 When the mixture has cooled, sift in the flour and cocoa powder. Dissolve the bicarbonate of soda in the milk, then add to the mixture with the egg and beat together until smooth.

4 Spoon the mixture evenly into the paper cases. Bake in the preheated oven for 15–20 minutes, or until well risen and firm to the touch. Transfer to a wire rack and leave to cool.

5 To make the topping, whisk the cream in a bowl until it holds its shape. Spoon a teaspoonful of cream on top of each cupcake, then dust with cocoa powder.

MINI CHERRY & ALMOND CUPCAKES

Makes: 18 **Prep: 25 mins, plus cooling** **Cook: 12–15 mins**

Ingredients

55 g/2 oz butter, softened

55 g/2 oz caster sugar

55 g/2 oz self-raising flour

25 g/1 oz ground almonds

1 egg, lightly beaten

a few drops of almond extract

18 fresh cherries, stalked and stoned, or 18 canned cherries

25 g/1 oz flaked almonds

icing sugar, sifted, for dusting

crème fraîche, to serve (optional)

Method

1 Preheat the oven to 180°C/350°F/Gas Mark 4. Line an 18-cup mini muffin tin with paper cases.

2 Place the butter, sugar, flour and ground almonds in a large bowl and, using an electric hand-held mixer, beat together until just smooth. Add the egg and almond extract and beat together briefly using a wooden spoon.

3 Spoon the mixture evenly into the paper cases, then lightly press a cherry into the centre of each cake. Sprinkle with the flaked almonds. Bake in the preheated oven for 12–15 minutes, or until well risen, golden and firm to the touch.

4 Transfer to a wire rack and leave to cool. Serve warm, dusted with sifted icing sugar and with spoonfuls of crème fraîche, if liked.

LEMON BUTTERFLY CUPCAKES

Makes: 12

Prep: 30 mins, plus cooling

Cook: 15–20 mins

Ingredients

115 g/4 oz self-raising flour

½ tsp baking powder

115 g/4 oz soft margarine

115 g/4 oz caster sugar

2 eggs

finely grated rind of ½ lemon

2 tbsp milk

icing sugar, for dusting

Frosting

85 g/3 oz butter, softened

175 g/6 oz icing sugar

1 tbsp lemon juice

Method

1 Preheat the oven to 190°C/375°F/Gas Mark 5. Line a 12-cup bun tin with paper cases.

2 Sift the flour and baking powder into a large bowl. Add the margarine, sugar, eggs, lemon rind and milk and, using an electric hand-held mixer, beat together until just smooth.

3 Spoon the mixture evenly into the paper cases. Bake in the preheated oven for 15–20 minutes, or until well risen, golden and firm to the touch. Transfer to a wire rack and leave to cool.

4 To make the frosting, put the butter in a bowl and beat until fluffy. Sift in the icing sugar, add the lemon juice and beat together until smooth and creamy.

5 Cut the top off each cake, using a serrated knife. Cut each cake top in half. Spread the frosting over the cut surface of each cake and push the two pieces of cake top into the frosting to form wings. Dust with sifted icing sugar before serving.

★ **Variation**

If you wanted a different flavour for the frosting, you could change the lemon juice to lime juice.

CLASSIC CUPCAKES

SPECIAL OCCASION CUPCAKES

BIRTHDAY PARTY CUPCAKES

Makes: 24

Prep: 40 mins, plus cooling

Cook: 15–20 mins

Ingredients

225 g/8 oz soft margarine

225 g/8 oz caster sugar

4 eggs

225 g/8 oz self-raising flour, sifted

a variety of small sweets, sugar-coated chocolates, dried fruit, edible sugar flower shapes, cake decorating sprinkles, sugar strands, and hundreds and thousands

candles and candleholders (optional)

Frosting

175 g/6 oz butter, softened

350 g/12 oz icing sugar

Method

1 Preheat the oven to 180°C/350°F/Gas Mark 4. Line two muffin tins with 24 paper cases.

2 Put the margarine, sugar, eggs and flour in a large bowl and, using an electric hand-held mixer, beat together until just smooth.

3 Spoon the mixture evenly into the paper cases. Bake in the preheated oven for 15–20 minutes, or until well risen, golden and firm to the touch. Transfer to a wire rack and leave to cool.

4 To make the frosting, put the butter in a bowl and beat until fluffy. Sift in the icing sugar and beat together until smooth and creamy. Spoon the frosting into a piping bag fitted with a large star nozzle. When the cupcakes are cool, pipe circles of frosting on top of each cupcake, then decorate as you choose. If desired, place a candle in the top of each.

★ Variation

These cupcakes can also be decorated with chocolate buttons and crumbled flaky chocolate for a chocolate lovers' birthday.

CHERRY SUNDAE CUPCAKES

Makes: 12

Prep: 30 mins, plus cooling

Cook: 30–35 mins

Ingredients

175 g/6 oz butter, softened, or soft margarine

175 g/6 oz caster sugar

3 eggs, lightly beaten

1 tsp vanilla extract

200 g/7 oz plain flour

1½ tsp baking powder

55 g/2 oz glacé cherries, chopped

Chocolate sauce

85 g/3 oz plain chocolate, broken into pieces

25 g/1 oz butter

1 tbsp golden syrup

To decorate

600 ml/1 pint double cream

2 tbsp toasted chopped mixed nuts

pink glimmer sugar

12 maraschino cherries

Method

1 Preheat the oven to 160°C/325°F/Gas Mark 3. Line a 12-cup bun tin with paper cases.

2 Place the butter and caster sugar in a large bowl and beat together until light and fluffy. Gradually beat in the eggs and vanilla extract. Sift in the flour and baking powder and, using a metal spoon, fold in gently. Fold in the glacé cherries.

3 Spoon the mixture evenly into the paper cases. Bake in the preheated oven for 25–30 minutes, or until well risen, golden and firm to the touch. Transfer to a wire rack and leave to cool.

4 To make the chocolate sauce, place the chocolate, butter and syrup in a heatproof bowl set over a saucepan of simmering water and heat until melted. Remove from the heat and stir until smooth. Leave to cool, stirring occasionally, for 20–30 minutes.

5 To decorate, whip the cream until holding firm peaks. Spoon into a piping bag fitted with a large star nozzle and pipe large swirls of cream on top of each cupcake. Drizzle over the chocolate sauce and sprinkle with the chopped nuts and pink sugar. Top each with a maraschino cherry.

SWEET SHOP CUPCAKES

Makes: 12

Prep: 25 mins, plus cooling

Cook: 18–22 mins

Ingredients

150 g/5½ oz butter, softened, or soft margarine

150 g/5½ oz caster sugar

3 eggs, lightly beaten

150 g/5½ oz self-raising flour

4 tsp strawberry-flavoured popping candy

sweets of your choice, to decorate (optional)

Frosting

175 g/6 oz butter, softened

2 tbsp milk

350 g/12 oz icing sugar

pink and yellow food colourings

Method

1 Preheat the oven to 180°C/350°F/Gas Mark 4. Line a 12-cup bun tin with paper cases.

2 Place the butter and caster sugar in a large bowl and beat together until light and fluffy. Gradually beat in the eggs. Sift in the flour and, using a metal spoon, fold in gently. Fold in half of the popping candy.

3 Spoon the mixture evenly into the paper cases. Bake in the preheated oven for 18–22 minutes, or until well risen, golden and firm to the touch. Transfer to a wire rack and leave to cool.

4 To make the frosting, place the butter in a bowl and beat until light and fluffy. Beat in the milk, then gradually sift in the icing sugar and continue beating for 2–3 minutes, or until the frosting is light and fluffy. Divide the frosting between two bowls and beat a little pink or yellow food colouring into each bowl.

5 Pipe or swirl the frosting on top of the cupcakes and decorate with the sweets, if using. Sprinkle the remaining popping candy over the top of the cupcakes just before serving.

SPECIAL OCCASION CUPCAKES

'99' CUPCAKES

Makes: 8

Prep: 25 mins, plus cooling

Cook: 20–25 mins

Ingredients

175 g/6 oz butter, softened, or soft margarine

175 g/6 oz caster sugar

3 eggs, lightly beaten

1 tsp vanilla extract

150 g/5½ oz self-raising flour

55 g/2 oz ground almonds

12 mini chocolate flakes, to decorate

hundreds and thousands, to decorate

Frosting

225 g/8 oz butter, softened

1 tbsp cream or milk

350 g/12 oz icing sugar

Method

1 Preheat the oven to 180°C/350°F/Gas Mark 4. Line a muffin tin with 8 paper cases.

2 Place the butter and caster sugar in a large bowl and beat together until light and fluffy. Gradually beat in the eggs and vanilla extract. Sift in the flour and, using a metal spoon, fold gently into the mixture with the ground almonds.

3 Spoon the mixture evenly into the paper cases. Bake in the preheated oven for 20–25 minutes, or until well risen, golden and firm to the touch. Transfer to a wire rack and leave to cool.

4 To make the frosting, place the butter in a bowl and beat with an electric hand-held mixer for 2–3 minutes, or until pale and creamy. Beat in the cream, then gradually sift in the icing sugar and continue beating for 2–3 minutes, or until the frosting is light and fluffy.

5 Spoon the frosting into a large piping bag fitted with a large star nozzle. Pipe swirls of frosting on top of each cupcake to resemble ice cream. Press a chocolate flake into each swirl of frosting and scatter with hundreds and thousands.

SPECIAL OCCASION CUPCAKES

CHEEKY MONKEY CUPCAKES

Makes: 12

Prep: 40 mins, plus cooling

Cook: 15–20 mins

Ingredients

115 g/4 oz butter, softened, or soft margarine

85 g/3 oz soft light brown sugar

1 tbsp honey

2 eggs, lightly beaten

100 g/3½ oz self-raising flour

2 tbsp cocoa powder

To decorate

350 g/12 oz ivory ready-to-roll fondant icing

brown food colouring

icing sugar, for dusting

2 tbsp chocolate spread

24 large chocolate buttons

white and black writing icing

12 brown candy-covered chocolate beans

Method

1 Preheat the oven to 180°C/350°F/Gas Mark 4. Line a 12-cup bun tin with paper cases.

2 Place the butter, brown sugar and honey in a large bowl and beat together until light and fluffy. Gradually beat in the eggs. Sift in the flour and cocoa powder and fold in gently.

3 Spoon the mixture evenly into the paper cases. Bake in the preheated oven for 15–20 minutes, or until well risen and firm to the touch. Transfer to a wire rack and leave to cool.

4 Colour two thirds of the ivory icing pale brown with food colouring. Roll out the brown fondant icing to a thickness of 5 mm/¼ inch on a surface dusted with icing sugar. Using a 7-cm/2¾-inch round cutter, stamp out 12 rounds. Roll out the remaining ivory fondant icing and, using the end of a large plain piping nozzle, cut out 24 small rounds. Re-roll the icing and cut out 12 ovals.

5 Spread each cupcake with chocolate spread and top with the brown icing. Attach two ivory rounds and one oval with a little water to create a monkey face. Using some of the writing icing, attach a chocolate button on either side for ears. Use the writing icings to pipe eyes and a mouth and place a chocolate bean in the centre of each face for a nose.

SPECIAL OCCASION CUPCAKES

2

5

5

LEMON MERINGUE PARTY CUPCAKES

Makes: 4   **Prep: 20 mins**   **Cook: 20 mins**

Ingredients

85 g/3 oz butter, softened, plus extra for greasing

85 g/3 oz caster sugar

finely grated rind and juice from ½ lemon

1 large egg, lightly beaten

85 g/3 oz self-raising flour

2 tbsp lemon curd

Meringue

2 egg whites

115 g/4 oz caster sugar

Method

1 Preheat the oven to 190°C/375°F/Gas Mark 5. Grease four 200-ml/7-fl oz ovenproof teacups or dishes (such as ramekins) with butter.

2 Put the butter, sugar and lemon rind in a bowl and beat together until light and fluffy. Gradually beat in the egg. Sift in the flour and, using a metal spoon, fold into the mixture with the lemon juice.

3 Spoon the mixture evenly into the cups or dishes. Put the cups or dishes on a baking sheet and bake in the preheated oven for 15 minutes, or until well risen, golden and firm to the touch.

4 Whilst the cupcakes are baking, make the meringue by putting the egg whites in a clean grease-free bowl and, using an electric hand-held mixer, whisk until stiff. Gradually whisk in the caster sugar to form a stiff and glossy meringue.

5 Spread the lemon curd over the hot cupcakes then swirl over the meringue. Return the cupcakes to the oven for 4–5 minutes, or until the meringue is golden. Serve immediately.

SPECIAL OCCASION CUPCAKES

MINI MAPLE & BANANA CUPCAKES

Makes: 12

Prep: 30 mins, plus cooling

Cook: 18–20 mins

Ingredients

1 small banana
2 tbsp maple syrup
2 tbsp milk
60 g/2¼ oz butter, softened
70 g/2½ oz caster sugar
1 egg, beaten
100 g/3½ oz self-raising flour
8 pecan or walnut halves, roughly chopped, to decorate

Frosting

150 g/5½ oz butter, softened
1 tsp vanilla extract
6 tbsp icing sugar
7 tbsp maple syrup

Method

1 Preheat the oven to 180°C/350°F/Gas Mark 4. Line a 12-cup mini muffin tin with paper cases.

2 In a small mixing bowl, mash the banana to a purée with a fork. Stir in the maple syrup and milk.

3 Put the butter and caster sugar in a separate mixing bowl and beat together with an electric hand-held mixer until light and fluffy. Gradually beat in the egg, a little at a time, adding a teaspoon of the flour if the mixture starts to separate.

4 Sift half of the flour into the bowl containing the butter mixture, then add half of the banana. Gently fold the ingredients together until only just mixed. Sift in the remaining flour, add the remaining banana mixture and fold in.

5 Spoon the mixture evenly into the paper cases. Bake in the preheated oven for 18–20 minutes, or until well risen, golden and firm to the touch. Transfer to a wire rack and leave to cool.

6 For the frosting, put the butter, vanilla, icing sugar and maple syrup in a bowl and beat until smooth and creamy. Put the frosting in a small paper piping bag fitted with a 1-cm/½-inch star nozzle and use to decorate the cupcakes. Scatter with the nuts.

SPECIAL OCCASION CUPCAKES

CHOCOLATE CURL CUPCAKES

Makes: 18

Prep: 25 mins,
plus cooling & chilling

Cook: 30 mins

Ingredients

85 g/3 oz butter, softened

100 g/3½ oz caster sugar

2 eggs, lightly beaten

2 tbsp milk

55 g/2 oz plain chocolate chips

225 g/8 oz self-raising flour

25 g/1 oz cocoa powder

chocolate curls, to decorate

Frosting

225 g/8 oz white chocolate, broken into pieces

150 g/5½ oz full-fat soft cheese

Method

1 Preheat the oven to 200°C/400°F/Gas Mark 6. Line two bun tins with 18 paper cases.

2 Put the butter and sugar in a bowl and beat together until light and fluffy. Gradually add the eggs, beating well after each addition. Add the milk, then fold in the chocolate chips. Sift the flour and cocoa powder together, then fold into the mixture.

3 Spoon the mixture evenly into the paper cases. Bake in the preheated oven for 20 minutes, or until well risen and firm to the touch. Transfer to a wire rack and leave to cool.

4 To make the frosting, place the chocolate in a heatproof bowl and set the bowl over a saucepan of simmering water until melted. Leave to cool slightly. Put the soft cheese in a bowl and beat until softened, then beat in the chocolate. Spread a little of the frosting over the top of each cupcake, then leave to chill in the refrigerator for 1 hour before serving. Serve decorated with the chocolate curls.

LOLLIPOP CUPCAKES

Makes: 12

Prep: 40 mins, plus cooling

Cook: 15–20 mins

Ingredients

115 g/4 oz butter, softened, or soft margarine

115 g/4 oz caster sugar

2 tsp finely grated orange rind

2 eggs, lightly beaten

115 g/4 oz self-raising flour

Frosting

115 g/4 oz butter, softened

2 tbsp orange juice

225 g/8 oz icing sugar

orange food colouring

To decorate

85 g/3 oz green ready-to-roll fondant icing

icing sugar, for dusting

red sugar sprinkles

12 small candy lollipops

Method

1 Preheat the oven to 180°C/350°F/Gas Mark 4. Line a 12-cup bun tin with paper cases.

2 Place the butter, caster sugar and orange rind in a large bowl and beat together until light and fluffy. Gradually beat in the eggs. Sift in the flour and, using a metal spoon, fold gently.

3 Spoon the mixture evenly into the paper cases. Bake in the preheated oven for 15–20 minutes, or until well risen, golden and firm to the touch. Transfer to a wire rack and leave to cool.

4 To make the frosting, place the butter and orange juice in a bowl and beat with an electric hand-held mixer for 2–3 minutes, or until pale and creamy. Gradually sift in the icing sugar and continue beating for 2–3 minutes, until the frosting is light and fluffy. Beat in a little orange food colouring.

5 Roll out the green fondant icing to a thickness of 5 mm/¼ inch on a surface lightly dusted with icing sugar. Using a small leaf cutter, stamp out 24 leaves. Swirl the frosting on the top of the cupcakes and edge with sugar sprinkles. Place a lollipop and two fondant leaves in the centre of each cupcake.

SPECIAL OCCASION CUPCAKES

PINK & GREEN CUPCAKES

Makes: 12

Prep: 30 mins, plus cooling

Cook: 20 mins

Ingredients

190 g/6¾ oz plain flour

1½ tsp baking powder

¼ tsp salt

115 g/4 oz butter, softened

200 g/7 oz caster sugar

2 tsp vanilla extract

2 large eggs, lightly beaten

125 ml/4 fl oz milk

pink food colouring

90 g/3¼ oz plain chocolate chips

Frosting

115 g/4 oz butter, softened

about 250 g/9 oz icing sugar (see method)

1 tbsp milk

1 tsp vanilla extract

pinch of salt

green food colouring

Method

1 Preheat the oven to 180°C/350°F/Gas Mark 4. Line a 12-cup bun tin with paper cases.

2 Sift together the flour, baking powder and salt in a bowl. Put the butter and caster sugar into a separate bowl and beat until light and fluffy. Add the vanilla extract, then add the eggs, a little at a time, beating after each addition. Add half of the flour mixture and the milk and beat until incorporated. Add the remaining flour mixture and mix.

3 Add several drops of food colouring and beat until evenly combined. Gradually add more colouring until a vibrant pink is achieved. Stir in the chocolate chips.

4 Spoon the mixture evenly into the paper cases. Bake in the preheated oven for 20 minutes, or until well risen and firm to the touch. Transfer to a wire rack and leave to cool.

5 To make the frosting, put the butter, icing sugar, milk, vanilla extract and salt into a bowl and beat with an electric hand-held mixer until well combined. Add more icing sugar, if necessary, to achieve a piping consistency.

6 Add several drops of food colouring and beat until evenly incorporated. Gradually add more colouring until a dark green colour is achieved. Transfer the frosting to a piping bag fitted with a star-shaped tip and pipe onto the cupcakes in swirls.

WEDDING DAY CUPCAKES

Makes: 30

Prep: 55 mins,
plus cooling & setting

Cook: 25–30 mins

Ingredients

350 g/12 oz self-raising flour

1 tsp baking powder

225 g/8 oz butter, softened, or soft margarine

225 g/8 oz caster sugar

finely grated rind of 1 large lemon

4 large eggs

2 tbsp milk

To decorate

650 g/1 lb 7 oz white ready-to-roll fondant icing

3 tbsp apricot jam, warmed and sieved

15 white fondant roses, dipped in edible silver glitter

2 tbsp egg white, lightly beaten

150 g/5½ oz icing sugar, sifted, plus extra for dusting

Method

1 Preheat the oven to 160°C/325°F/Gas Mark 3. Line three bun tins with 30 paper cases.

2 Sift the flour and baking powder into a large bowl. Add the butter, caster sugar, lemon rind, eggs and milk and, using an electric hand-held mixer, beat together until just smooth.

3 Spoon the mixture evenly into the paper cases. Bake in the preheated oven for 20–25 minutes, or until well risen, golden and firm to the touch. Transfer to a wire rack and leave to cool.

4 Roll out the white fondant icing to a thickness of 5 mm/¼ inch on a surface lightly dusted with icing sugar. Using a 6-cm/2½-inch cutter, stamp out 30 rounds, re-rolling the icing as necessary. Brush each cupcake lightly with a little of the jam and gently press an icing round on top. Gently press a fondant rose into the centre of half the iced cupcakes.

5 Place the egg white in a bowl and gradually beat in the icing sugar to make a smooth icing. Spoon the icing into a small piping bag fitted with a fine writing nozzle. Pipe a wavy line of icing all over the surface of each plain cupcake. Try not to let the lines touch or cross and keep an even pressure on the piping bag so that the lines are of the same thickness. Leave to set.

SPECIAL OCCASION CUPCAKES

ROSE PETAL CUPCAKES

Makes: 12

Prep: 25 mins, plus cooling

Cook: 12–15 mins

Ingredients

115 g/4 oz butter, softened

115 g/4 oz caster sugar

2 eggs, lightly beaten

1 tbsp milk

few drops of rose oil extract

¼ tsp vanilla extract

175 g/6 oz self-raising flour

crystallized rose petals, to decorate

Frosting

85 g/3 oz butter, softened

175 g/6 oz icing sugar

pink food colouring (optional)

Method

1 Preheat the oven to 200°C/400°F/Gas Mark 6. Line a 12-cup bun tin with paper cases.

2 Put the butter and sugar in a bowl and beat together until light and fluffy. Gradually add the eggs, beating well after each addition. Stir in the milk, rose oil and vanilla extract then sift in the flour and fold in using a metal spoon.

3 Spoon the mixture evenly into the paper cases. Bake in the preheated oven for 12–15 minutes, or until well risen, golden and firm to the touch. Transfer to a wire rack and leave to cool.

4 To make the frosting, put the butter in a large bowl and beat until fluffy. Sift in the icing sugar and mix well together. If wished, add a few drops of pink food colouring to complement the rose petals.

5 When the cupcakes are cool, put a dot of frosting on top of each cake. Top with 1–2 crystallized rose petals to decorate.

SPECIAL OCCASION CUPCAKES

LOVE HEART CUPCAKES

Makes: 6

Prep: 40 mins,
plus drying & cooling

Cook: 25–30 mins

Ingredients

85 g/3 oz butter, softened

85 g/3 oz caster sugar

½ tsp vanilla extract

2 eggs, lightly beaten

70 g/2½ oz plain flour

1 tbsp cocoa powder

1 tsp baking powder

6 sugar flowers, to decorate

Marzipan hearts

35 g/1¼ oz marzipan

red food colouring

icing sugar, for dusting

Frosting

55 g/2 oz butter, softened

115 g/4 oz icing sugar

25 g/1 oz melted chocolate

Method

1 To make the hearts, knead the marzipan until pliable, then add a few drops of red colouring and knead until evenly coloured. Roll out the marzipan to a thickness of 5 mm/¼ inch on a surface dusted with icing sugar. Using a small heart-shaped cutter, cut out 6 hearts. Place these on a tray, lined with greaseproof paper and dusted with sifted icing sugar, and leave to dry for 3–4 hours.

2 To make the cupcakes, preheat the oven to 180°C/350°F/ Gas Mark 4. Line a muffin tin with 6 paper cases.

3 Put the butter, sugar and vanilla extract in a bowl and beat together until light and fluffy. Gradually add the eggs, beating well after each addition. Sift in the flour, cocoa powder and baking powder and, using a large metal spoon, fold into the mixture. Spoon the mixture evenly into the paper cases. Bake in the preheated oven for 20–25 minutes, or until well risen and firm to the touch. Transfer to a wire rack and leave to cool.

4 To make the frosting, put the butter in a large bowl and beat until fluffy. Sift in the icing sugar and beat together until smooth. Add the melted chocolate and beat until well mixed. Spread some frosting over each cupcake and decorate with a marzipan heart and a sugar flower.

SPECIAL OCCASION CUPCAKES

WEDDING FAVOUR CUPCAKES

Makes: 12

Prep: 35 mins, plus cooling & setting

Cook: 20–25 mins

Ingredients

115 g/4 oz butter, softened

100 g/3½ oz caster sugar

2 eggs, lightly beaten

140 g/5 oz self-raising flour

½ tsp vanilla extract

1–2 tbsp milk

To decorate

icing sugar, for dusting

225 g/8 oz white ready-to-roll fondant icing

3 tbsp runny honey, warmed

2–3 drops pink food colouring

green writing icing

Method

1 Preheat the oven to 200°C/400°F/Gas Mark 6. Line a 12-cup muffin tin with paper cases.

2 Place the butter and caster sugar in a bowl and beat together until light and fluffy. Gradually add the eggs, beating well after each addition. Sift in the flour and fold in gently using a metal spoon. Stir in the vanilla extract and milk.

3 Spoon the mixture evenly into the paper cases. Bake in the preheated oven for 15–20 minutes, or until well risen, golden and firm to the touch. Transfer to a wire rack and leave to cool.

4 Dust the work surface with icing sugar. Roll out all but one eighth of the fondant icing to 20 x 28 cm/8 x 11 inches. Use a biscuit cutter to stamp out 12 rounds. Brush the cake tops with honey and stick the rounds onto the cupcakes.

5 For the rosebuds, knead the remaining icing with the food colouring. Roll out 12 strips of icing to 1 x 6 cm/½ x 2½ inches. Roll up and stick on top with honey. Draw on a stalk with the writing icing. Leave to set.

SPECIAL OCCASION CUPCAKES

ANNIVERSARY CUPCAKES

Makes: 24

Prep: 25 mins,
plus cooling

Cook: 15–20 mins

Ingredients

225 g/8 oz butter, softened

225 g/8 oz caster sugar

1 tsp vanilla extract

4 large eggs, lightly beaten

225 g/8 oz self-raising flour

5 tbsp milk

25 g/1 oz silver or gold
dragées, to decorate

Frosting

175 g/6 oz butter

350 g/12 oz icing sugar

Method

1 Preheat the oven to 180°C/350°F/Gas Mark 4.
  Line two muffin tins with 24 paper cases.

2 Put the butter, sugar and vanilla extract in a bowl
  and beat together until light and fluffy. Gradually
  add the eggs, beating well after each addition.
  Sift in the flour and, using a large metal spoon,
  fold into the mixture with the milk.

3 Spoon the mixture evenly into the paper cases.
  Bake in the preheated oven for 15–20 minutes,
  or until well risen, golden and firm to the touch.
  Transfer to a wire rack and leave to cool.

4 To make the frosting, put the butter in a bowl and
  beat until fluffy. Sift in the icing sugar and beat
  together. Put the frosting in a piping bag, fitted
  with a star-shaped nozzle.

5 When the cupcakes are cool, pipe circles of
  frosting on top of each cupcake to cover the
  tops. Sprinkle over the silver or gold dragées
  before serving.

SPECIAL OCCASION CUPCAKES

DATE NIGHT MUDSLIDE CUPCAKES

Makes: 12

Prep: 30 mins, plus cooling

Cook: 25 mins

Ingredients

125 g/4½ oz plain flour

60 g/2¼ oz cocoa powder

1½ tsp baking powder

¼ tsp salt

115 g/4 oz butter, softened

200 g/7 oz caster sugar

2 tsp vanilla extract

2 large eggs, lightly beaten

125 ml/4 fl oz double cream

40 g/1½ oz plain chocolate chips, plus extra for decorating

Frosting

60 g/2¼ oz butter, softened

about 250 g/9 oz icing sugar (see method)

2 tbsp milk

3 tbsp Irish cream liqueur

1 tsp vanilla extract

Chocolate sauce

55 g/2 oz plain chocolate, broken into pieces

4 tbsp double cream

15 g/½ oz butter

pinch of salt

Method

1 Preheat the oven to 180°C/350°F/Gas Mark 4. Line a 12-cup bun tin with paper cases.

2 Sift together the flour, cocoa powder, baking powder and salt in a bowl. Put the butter and caster sugar into a separate bowl and beat until light and fluffy. Add the vanilla extract, then add the eggs, a little at a time, beating after each addition. Add half of the flour mixture and the cream, and beat until incorporated. Add the remaining flour mixture and mix. Stir in the chocolate chips.

3 Spoon the mixture evenly into the paper cases. Bake in the preheated oven for 20 minutes, or until well risen and firm to the touch. Transfer to a wire rack and leave to cool.

4 To make the frosting, put the butter into a bowl and beat with an electric hand-held mixer until it is light and creamy. Add the icing sugar, milk, liqueur and vanilla extract. Beat together until well combined. Add more icing sugar, if necessary, to achieve a piping consistency. Spoon the frosting into a piping bag fitted with a star-shaped tip and pipe onto the cupcakes.

5 To make the chocolate sauce, place the chocolate, cream, butter and salt in a heatproof bowl set over a saucepan of gently simmering water and stir until the chocolate has completely melted. Set aside to cool for at least 15 minutes. To serve, lightly drizzle the chocolate sauce over the frosted cupcakes and sprinkle with chocolate chips.

I LOVE YOU CUPCAKES

Makes: 10

Prep: 45 mins, plus cooling

Cook: 20–25 mins

Ingredients

115 g/4 oz butter, softened, or soft margarine

115 g/4 oz caster sugar

1 tsp almond extract

2 large eggs, lightly beaten

115 g/4 oz self-raising flour

25 g/1 oz ground almonds

2 tbsp milk

3 tbsp raspberry jam

To decorate

75 g/2¾ oz red ready-to-roll fondant icing

150 g/5½ oz white ready-to-roll fondant icing

1 tbsp egg white, lightly beaten

85 g/3 oz icing sugar, sifted, plus extra for dusting

Method

1 Preheat the oven to 180°C/350°F/Gas Mark 4. Line a muffin tin with 10 paper cases.

2 Place the butter, caster sugar and almond extract in a large bowl and beat together until light and fluffy. Gradually beat in the eggs. Sift in the flour and, using a metal spoon, fold in gently with the ground almonds. Add the milk and fold gently into the mixture.

3 Spoon the mixture evenly into the paper cases. Bake in the preheated oven for 20–25 minutes, or until well risen, golden and firm to the touch. Transfer to a wire rack and leave to cool.

4 Using a small knife, scoop a little of the sponge out from each cake. Place ½ teaspoon of the jam into each hollow and replace the piece of sponge on top.

5 Roll out a small piece of the red fondant icing and, using a small heart cutter, stamp out two hearts. Lightly knead the remaining red fondant icing into the white fondant icing to create a marbled effect. Roll out to a thickness of 5 mm/¼ inch on a surface lightly dusted with icing sugar. Use a 7-cm/2¾-inch cutter to stamp out 10 rounds. Brush the tops of the cupcakes with the remaining jam and place the icing rounds on top.

SPECIAL OCCASION CUPCAKES

6 Place the egg white in a bowl and gradually beat in the icing sugar to make a smooth icing. Spoon the icing into a small piping bag fitted with a fine writing nozzle. Pipe each of the letters I, Y, O and U on two cupcakes and attach the fondant hearts with a dab of water to the two remaining cupcakes.

NEW BABY CUPCAKES

Makes: 12

Prep: 50 mins, plus cooling

Cook: 20–25 mins

Ingredients

115 g/4 oz self-raising flour

¼ tsp baking powder

115 g/4 oz butter, softened, or soft margarine

115 g/4 oz caster sugar

2 eggs

1 tbsp milk

1 tsp vanilla extract

To decorate

150 g/5½ oz white ready-to-roll fondant icing

icing sugar, for dusting

150 g/5½ oz pale blue or pink ready-to-roll fondant icing

1 tbsp apricot jam, warmed and sieved

white writing icing

Method

1 Preheat the oven to 180°C/350°F/Gas Mark 4. Line a 12-cup bun tin with paper cases.

2 Sift the flour and baking powder into a large bowl. Add the butter, caster sugar, eggs, milk and vanilla extract and, using an electric hand-held mixer, beat together until just smooth.

3 Spoon the mixture evenly into the paper cases. Bake in the preheated oven for 15–20 minutes, or until well risen, golden and firm to the touch. Transfer to a wire rack and leave to cool.

4 Roll out the white fondant icing to a thickness of 5 mm/¼ inch on a surface lightly dusted with icing sugar. Using a 6-cm/2½-inch cutter, stamp out 6 rounds. Repeat with the blue or pink fondant icing. Brush each cupcake lightly with a little of the jam and gently press an icing round on top.

5 Re-roll the blue or pink fondant icing trimmings. Use a small teddy bear cutter to stamp out two teddy bears. Use a tiny flower cutter to stamp out four flowers.

6 Re-roll the white fondant icing trimmings. Use a small flower cutter to stamp out two small flowers. Use a 4-cm/1½-inch fluted cutter to stamp out two rounds, then cut away a small oval from each round to resemble a baby's bib. Use a

SPECIAL OCCASION CUPCAKES

2.5-cm/1-inch cutter to stamp out two rounds and mark with the end of a paintbrush to resemble buttons. Shape four booties and two ducks from the remaining fondant icing trimmings.

7   Attach all the decorations to the top of the cupcakes with a little water. Use the writing icing to add the finishing touches, such as bows on the booties or eyes for the duck.

EASTER CUPCAKES

Makes: 12

Prep: 25 mins, plus cooling

Cook: 15–20 mins

Ingredients

115 g/4 oz butter, softened

115 g/4 oz caster sugar

2 eggs, lightly beaten

85 g/3 oz self-raising flour

25 g/1 oz cocoa powder

260 g/9¼ oz mini chocolate candy-shell eggs, to decorate

Frosting

85 g/3 oz butter, softened

175 g/6 oz icing sugar

1 tbsp milk

2–3 drops of vanilla extract

Method

1 Preheat the oven to 180°C/350°F/Gas Mark 4. Line a 12-cup bun tin with paper cases.

2 Put the butter and sugar in a bowl and beat together until light and fluffy. Gradually add the eggs, beating well after each addition. Sift in the flour and cocoa powder and, using a large metal spoon, fold into the mixture.

3 Spoon the mixture evenly into the paper cases. Bake in the preheated oven for 15–20 minutes, or until well risen and firm to the touch. Transfer to a wire rack and leave to cool.

4 To make the frosting, put the butter in a bowl and beat until fluffy. Sift in the icing sugar and beat together until well mixed, adding the milk and vanilla extract. Put the frosting in a piping bag fitted with a large star-shaped nozzle. When the cupcakes are cool, pipe circles of frosting on top of the cupcakes to form nests. Decorate with chocolate eggs.

3

4

4

CHOCOLATE ORANGE CUPCAKES

Makes: 16

Prep: 20 mins,
plus cooling & setting

Cook: 25 mins

Ingredients

115 g/4 oz butter, softened

115 g/4 oz golden caster sugar

finely grated rind and juice of ½ orange

2 eggs, lightly beaten

115 g/4 oz self-raising flour

25 g/1 oz plain chocolate, grated

Frosting

115 g/4 oz plain chocolate, broken into pieces

25 g/1 oz butter

1 tbsp golden syrup

thin strips candied orange peel, to decorate

Method

1 Preheat the oven to 180°C/350°F/Gas Mark 4. Line two bun tins with 16 paper cases.

2 Put the butter, sugar and orange rind in a bowl and beat together until light and fluffy. Gradually beat in the eggs, beating well after each addition. Sift in the flour and, using a metal spoon, fold gently into the mixture with the orange juice and grated chocolate.

3 Spoon the mixture evenly into the paper cases. Bake in the preheated oven for 20 minutes, or until well risen and firm to the touch. Transfer to a wire rack and leave to cool.

4 To make the frosting, place the chocolate in a heatproof bowl and add the butter and syrup. Set the bowl over a saucepan of simmering water and heat until melted. Remove from the heat and stir until smooth. Cool until the frosting is thick enough to spread. Spread over the cupcakes and decorate each cupcake with a few strips of candied orange peel. Leave to set.

AUTUMN BLACKBERRY CRUMBLE CUPCAKES

Makes: 6　　　　**Prep: 20 mins**　　　　**Cook: 25–30 mins**

Ingredients

115 g/4 oz self-raising flour

½ tsp baking powder

115 g/4 oz butter, softened, plus extra for greasing

115 g/4 oz caster sugar

2 eggs

175 g/6 oz blackberries

whipped cream or custard, to serve

Crumble topping

85 g/3 oz self-raising flour

55 g/2 oz demerara sugar

55 g/2 oz butter, chilled and diced

Method

1　Preheat the oven to 190°C/375°F/Gas Mark 5. Grease six 200-ml/7-fl oz ovenproof teacups or dishes (such as ramekins) with butter.

2　To make the crumble topping, mix the flour and demerara sugar in a bowl. Add the butter and rub in until the mixture resembles coarse breadcrumbs.

3　To make the cupcakes, sift the flour and baking powder into a bowl. Add the butter, caster sugar and eggs and, using an electric hand-held mixer, beat together until just smooth. Spoon the mixture evenly into the cups or dishes and level the surface. Top with the blackberries. Spoon the crumble topping over the blackberries.

4　Put the cups or dishes on a baking sheet and bake in the preheated oven for 25–30 minutes, or until the crumble topping is golden brown. Serve warm with whipped cream.

SUMMER GARDEN CUPCAKES

Makes: 8

Prep: 45 mins, plus cooling

Cook: 15–20 mins

Ingredients

115 g/4 oz butter, softened, or soft margarine

115 g/4 oz caster sugar

2 tsp rose water

2 large eggs, lightly beaten

115 g/4 oz self-raising flour

To decorate

115 g/4 oz pink ready-to-roll fondant icing

icing sugar, for dusting

85 g/3 oz white ready-to-roll fondant icing

85 g/3 oz blue ready-to-roll fondant icing

yellow writing icing

Frosting

175 g/6 oz butter, softened

6 tbsp double cream

350 g/12 oz icing sugar

green food colouring

Method

1 Preheat the oven to 180°C/350°F/Gas Mark 4. Line a bun tin with 8 paper cases.

2 Place the butter, caster sugar and rose water in a large bowl and beat together until light and fluffy. Gradually beat in the eggs. Sift in the flour and, using a metal spoon, fold in gently.

3 Spoon the mixture evenly into the paper cases. Bake in the preheated oven for 15–20 minutes, or until well risen, golden and firm to the touch. Transfer to a wire rack and leave to cool.

4 Roll out the pink fondant icing to a thickness of 5 mm/¼ inch on a surface lightly dusted with icing sugar. Using a small butterfly cutter, stamp out 16 butterflies. Roll out the white and blue fondant icings to the same thickness and, using a small daisy cutter, stamp out about 40 flowers, re-rolling the icing and using the trimmings as necessary. Use the yellow writing icing to pipe centres in the flowers.

5 To make the frosting, place the butter in a large bowl and beat with an electric hand-held mixer for 2–3 minutes, or until light and creamy. Slowly beat in the cream, then gradually sift in the icing sugar and continue beating for 2–3 minutes, or until the frosting is light and fluffy. Beat in a little

of the green food colouring, in order to create a light green colour for the frosting.

6 Spoon the frosting into a large piping bag fitted with a large star nozzle. Pipe swirls of frosting on top of each cupcake. Decorate with the fondant butterflies and flowers.

GINGERBREAD CUPCAKES

Makes: 30

Prep: 30 mins, plus cooling

Cook: 15–20 mins

Ingredients

175 g/6 oz plain flour

1 tbsp baking powder

2 tsp ground ginger

1 tsp ground cinnamon

175 g/6 oz butter, softened

175 g/6 oz dark muscovado sugar

3 eggs

1 tsp vanilla extract

chopped crystallized ginger, to decorate

Frosting

85 g/3 oz butter, softened

150 g/5½ oz icing sugar, sifted

3 tbsp orange juice

Method

1 Preheat the oven to 190°C/375°F/Gas Mark 5. Line three bun tins with 30 paper cases.

2 Sift the flour, baking powder, ginger and cinnamon into a large bowl and add the butter, muscovado sugar, eggs and vanilla extract. Beat with an electric hand-held mixer until the mixture is just smooth.

3 Spoon the mixture evenly into the paper cases. Bake in the preheated oven for 15–20 minutes, or until well risen, golden and firm to the touch. Transfer to a wire rack and leave to cool.

4 For the frosting, beat together the butter, icing sugar and orange juice until smooth. Spoon a little frosting on top of each cupcake and top with the crystallized ginger.

SPECIAL OCCASION CUPCAKES

HALLOWEEN CUPCAKES

Makes: 12

Prep: 40 mins, plus cooling

Cook: 15–20 mins

Ingredients

115 g/4 oz soft margarine

115 g/4 oz caster sugar

2 eggs

115 g/4 oz self-raising flour, sifted

To decorate

200 g/7 oz orange ready-to-roll fondant icing

icing sugar, for dusting

55 g/2 oz black ready-to-roll fondant icing

black writing icing

yellow writing icing

Method

1 Preheat the oven to 180°C/350°F/Gas Mark 4. Line a 12-cup bun tin with paper cases.

2 Put the margarine, sugar, eggs and flour in a bowl and, using an electric hand-held mixer, beat together until just smooth.

3 Spoon the mixture evenly into the paper cases. Bake in the preheated oven for 15–20 minutes, or until well risen, golden and firm to the touch. Transfer to a wire rack and leave to cool.

4 When the cupcakes are cool, knead the orange icing until pliable, then roll out on a surface lightly dusted with sifted icing sugar. Using the palm of your hand, lightly rub sifted icing sugar into the icing to prevent it from spotting. Using a 5.5-cm/2¼-inch plain round cutter, cut out 12 circles, re-rolling the icing as necessary. Place a circle on top of each cupcake.

5 Roll out the black icing on a surface lightly dusted with icing sugar. Using the palm of your hand, lightly rub icing sugar into the icing to prevent it from spotting. Using a 3-cm/1¼-inch plain round cutter, cut out 12 circles and place them on the centre of the cupcakes. Using black writing icing, pipe eight legs on to each spider and using yellow writing icing, draw two eyes and a mouth.

SPECIAL OCCASION CUPCAKES

GHOSTLY GHOUL CUPCAKES

Makes: 6

Prep: 50 mins, plus cooling & chilling

Cook: 15–20 mins

Ingredients

85 g/3 oz butter, softened, or soft margarine

85 g/3 oz dark muscovado sugar

1 tbsp black treacle

2 large eggs, lightly beaten

140 g/5 oz plain flour

2 tsp ground mixed spice

¾ tsp bicarbonate of soda

Frosting

85 g/3 oz butter, softened

1 tbsp dulce de leche

175 g/6 oz icing sugar

To decorate

350 g/12 oz white ready-to-roll fondant icing

icing sugar, for dusting

black writing icing

Method

1 Preheat the oven to 180°C/350°F/Gas Mark 4. Put 12 paper cases in a bun tray and 6 paper cases in a mini muffin tray.

2 Place the butter, muscovado sugar and treacle in a bowl and beat together until light and fluffy. Gradually beat in the eggs. Sift in the flour, mixed spice and bicarbonate of soda and, using a metal spoon, fold in gently.

3 Spoon the mixture evenly into the paper cases. Bake the mini muffins in the preheated oven for 10–12 minutes and the cupcakes for 15–20 minutes, or until well risen and firm to the touch. Transfer to a wire rack and leave to cool.

4 To make the frosting, place the butter and dulce de leche in a bowl and beat with an electric hand-held mixer for 2–3 minutes, or until pale and creamy. Gradually sift in the icing sugar and beat until smooth.

5 To assemble, remove the paper cases from half of the cupcakes and all the mini muffins. Level the tops of all the cakes if necessary. Spread a layer of the frosting over the top of the remaining cupcakes. Top each with an upturned cupcake and an upturned mini muffin. Spread the frosting all over the stacked cakes. Chill in the refrigerator for 30 minutes.

SPECIAL OCCASION CUPCAKES

6 Take 50 g/1¾ oz of the white fondant icing and roll into six small balls. Place one on top of each of the stacked cakes. Divide the remaining fondant into six pieces and roll out each piece on a surface lightly dusted with icing sugar to a 14-cm/5½-inch round with a thickness of about 3 mm/⅛ inch. Drape over the cupcakes. Use the black writing icing to pipe ghost faces on each cupcake.

CHRISTMAS HOLLY CUPCAKES

Makes: 16

Prep: 45 mins,
plus cooling

Cook: 20 mins

Ingredients

125 g/4½ oz butter, softened

200 g/7 oz caster sugar

4–6 drops almond extract

4 eggs, lightly beaten

150 g/5½ oz self-raising flour, sifted

175 g/6 oz ground almonds

To decorate

450 g/1 lb white ready-to-roll fondant icing

icing sugar, for dusting

55 g/2 oz green ready-to-roll fondant icing

25 g/1 oz red ready-to-roll fondant icing

Method

1. Preheat the oven to 180°C/350°F/Gas Mark 4. Line two muffin tins with 16 paper cases.

2. Put the butter, sugar and almond extract in a bowl and beat together until light and fluffy. Gradually add the eggs, beating well after each addition. Add the flour and fold it into the mixture, then fold in the ground almonds.

3. Spoon the mixture evenly into the paper cases. Bake in the preheated oven for 20 minutes, or until well risen, golden and firm to the touch. Transfer to a wire rack and leave to cool.

4. When the cupcakes are cool, knead the white icing until pliable, then roll out on a surface lightly dusted with sifted icing sugar. Using a 7-cm/2¾-inch plain round cutter, cut out 16 circles, re-rolling the icing as necessary. Place a circle on top of each cupcake.

5. Roll out the green icing on a surface lightly dusted with sifted icing sugar. Rub icing sugar into the icing to prevent it from spotting. Using a holly-leaf-shaped cutter, cut out 32 leaves, re-rolling the icing as necessary. Brush each leaf with a little cooled boiled water and place two leaves on top of each cupcake. Roll the red icing to form 48 berries and place in the centre of the leaves, to decorate.

SPECIAL OCCASION CUPCAKES

CHRISTMAS BAUBLE CUPCAKES

Makes: 14

Prep: 30 mins, plus soaking & cooling

Cook: 15–20 mins

Ingredients

115 g/4 oz mixed dried fruit

1 tsp finely grated orange rind

2 tbsp brandy or orange juice

85 g/3 oz butter, softened

85 g/3 oz light soft brown sugar

1 large egg, lightly beaten

115 g/4 oz self-raising flour

1 tsp ground mixed spice

1 tbsp silver dragées, to decorate

Topping

85 g/3 oz icing sugar

2 tbsp orange juice

Method

1 Put the mixed fruit, orange rind and brandy in a small bowl. Cover and leave to soak for 1 hour.

2 Preheat the oven to 190°C/375°F/Gas Mark 5. Line two bun tins with 14 paper cases.

3 Put the butter and sugar in a large bowl and beat together until light and fluffy. Gradually beat in the egg. Sift in the flour and mixed spice and, using a metal spoon, fold them into the mixture followed by the soaked fruit.

4 Spoon the mixture evenly into the paper cases. Bake in the preheated oven for 15–20 minutes, or until well risen, golden and firm to the touch. Transfer to a wire rack and leave to cool.

5 To make the topping, sift the icing sugar into a bowl and gradually mix in enough orange juice until the mixture is smooth and thick enough to coat the back of a wooden spoon. Using a teaspoon, drizzle the topping in a zig-zag pattern over the cupcakes. Decorate with the silver dragées. Leave to set.

SNOWMAN CUPCAKES

Makes: 10

Prep: 40 mins, plus cooling

Cook: 15–20 mins

Ingredients

115 g/4 oz butter, softened, or soft margarine

115 g/4 oz caster sugar

2 large eggs, lightly beaten

115 g/4 oz self-raising flour

85 g/3 oz desiccated coconut

2 tbsp milk

Frosting

55 g/2 oz butter, softened

2 tbsp double cream

115 g/4 oz icing sugar

To decorate

55 g/2 oz black ready-to-roll fondant icing

icing sugar, for dusting

sliced glacé cherries, angelica, chocolate chips and orange jelly diamonds

Method

1 Preheat the oven to 180°C/350°F/Gas Mark 4. Line a bun tin with 10 paper cases.

2 Place the butter and caster sugar in a large bowl and beat until light and fluffy. Gradually beat in the eggs. Sift in the flour and fold in. Fold in 55 g/2 oz of the coconut and the milk. Spoon evenly into the paper cases. Bake for 15–20 minutes, or until well risen, golden and firm to the touch. Transfer to a wire rack and leave to cool.

3 To make the frosting, beat the butter with an electric hand-held mixer for 2–3 minutes, or until creamy. Beat in the cream, then sift in the icing sugar and beat for 2–3 minutes.

4 Spread the frosting over the cupcakes. Sprinkle over the remaining coconut. Roll out the black fondant on a dusted surface and cut out 10 hat shapes. Decorate each hat with glacé cherry and angelica to resemble holly and berries. Gently press two chocolate chips, a jelly diamond and a rolled strip of black fondant on top of each cupcake for the snowman's face.

★ Variation

You could also add scarves to the snowmen, if you have any leftover black fondant icing.

SPECIAL OCCASION CUPCAKES

FUN FLAVOUR CUPCAKES

MARGARITA CUPCAKES

Makes: 12

Prep: 30 mins, plus cooling

Cook: 25 mins

Ingredients

190 g/6¾ oz plain flour

1½ tsp baking powder

¼ tsp salt

115 g/4 oz butter, softened

200 g/7 oz caster sugar

2 tsp vanilla extract

2 large eggs, lightly beaten

90 ml/3 fl oz milk

3 tbsp tequila

finely grated rind and juice of 1 lime

Frosting

3 large egg whites

150 g/5½ oz granulated sugar

225 g/8 oz butter, softened

4 tbsp triple sec

finely grated rind of 1 lime

green food colouring

Method

1 Preheat the oven to 180°C/350°F/Gas Mark 4. Line a 12-cup bun tin with paper cases.

2 Sift the flour, baking powder and salt in a bowl. Put the butter and caster sugar into a bowl and beat until light and fluffy. Add the vanilla and the eggs, a little at a time, beating after each addition. Add half of the flour mixture and the milk, tequila, lime rind and juice, and beat until combined. Fold in the remaining flour mixture.

3 Spoon the mixture evenly into the paper cases. Bake in the preheated oven for 20 minutes, or until well risen. Transfer to a wire rack to cool.

4 To make the frosting, put the egg whites and granulated sugar in a heatproof bowl set over a saucepan of simmering water and whisk until the sugar has dissolved. Remove from the heat and whisk the mixture for 4–5 minutes. Add the butter, a little at a time, and continue to whisk until it holds stiff peaks. Add the triple sec, lime rind and 2 drops of food colouring and stir until combined. Spoon the frosting into a piping bag fitted with a star-shaped tip and pipe onto the cupcakes.

★ **Variation**

If you don't have any tequila, then rum works equally well in these cupcakes.

FUN FLAVOUR CUPCAKES

PIÑA COLADA CUPCAKES

Makes: 12

Prep: 30 mins, plus cooling

Cook: 25 mins

Ingredients

190 g/6¾ oz plain flour

1½ tsp baking powder

¼ tsp salt

115 g/4 oz butter, softened

200 g/7 oz caster sugar

2 large eggs, lightly beaten

2 tbsp white rum

125 ml/4 fl oz milk

85 g/3 oz canned pineapple, drained and crushed with a fork

60 g/2¼ oz toasted desiccated coconut

12 cocktail umbrellas, to decorate

Frosting

4 large egg whites

200 g/7 oz granulated sugar

¼ tsp cream of tartar

1 tbsp coconut extract

2 tbsp coconut cream

Method

1 Preheat the oven to 180°C/350°F/Gas Mark 4. Line a 12-cup bun tin with paper cases.

2 Sift together the flour, baking powder and salt in a bowl. Put the butter and caster sugar into a separate bowl and beat until light and fluffy. Add the eggs, a little at a time, beating after each addition. Add the rum, milk and half of the flour mixture, and beat until combined. Add the remaining flour mixture and mix. Stir in the pineapple.

3 Spoon the mixture evenly into the paper cases. Bake in the preheated oven for 20 minutes, or until well risen, golden and firm to the touch. Transfer to a wire rack and leave to cool.

4 To make the frosting, put the egg whites, granulated sugar and cream of tartar in a heatproof bowl set over a saucepan of gently simmering water and whisk until the sugar has dissolved. Remove from the heat and whisk the mixture for 4–5 minutes, or until it holds stiff peaks. Add the coconut extract and coconut cream and stir until combined. Spoon the frosting into a piping bag fitted with a star-shaped tip and pipe onto the cupcakes. Sprinkle with toasted desiccated coconut and decorate each cupcake with a cocktail umbrella.

MAPLE & BACON CUPCAKES

Makes: 12

Prep: 35 mins, plus cooling

Cook: 50–55 mins

Ingredients

190 g/6¾ oz plain flour
1½ tsp baking powder
¼ tsp salt
115 g/4 oz butter, softened
100 g/3½ oz caster sugar
125 ml/4 fl oz maple syrup
1 tsp vanilla extract
2 large eggs, lightly beaten
125 ml/4 fl oz milk

Candied bacon

8 rashers unsmoked streaky bacon
55 g/2 oz soft light brown sugar

Frosting

4 large egg whites
200 g/7 oz granulated sugar
¼ tsp cream of tartar
2 tbsp maple syrup
2 tsp maple extract

Method

1 Preheat the oven to 180°C/350°F/Gas Mark 4. Line a 12-cup bun tin with paper cases.

2 To make the candied bacon, line a baking sheet with foil. Place the bacon on the prepared sheet and sprinkle half of the sugar over. Turn and repeat. Bake in the preheated oven for 25–30 minutes, or until the bacon is crisp (do not switch off the oven). Transfer to kitchen paper and leave to cool. Reserve 4 whole rashers of bacon for decoration and crumble the remaining bacon.

3 Sift together the flour, baking powder and salt in a bowl. Put the butter and caster sugar into a separate bowl and beat until light and fluffy. Add the maple syrup and vanilla extract, then add the eggs, a little at a time, beating after each addition. Add half of the flour mixture and the milk and beat until combined. Add the remaining flour mixture and mix. Add the crumbled candied bacon to the mixture and fold in.

4 Spoon the mixture evenly into the paper cases. Bake in the preheated oven for 20 minutes, or until well risen, golden and firm to the touch. Transfer to a wire rack and leave to cool.

5 To make the frosting, put the egg whites, granulated sugar and cream of tartar in a heatproof bowl set over a saucepan of gently simmering water and whisk until the sugar is completely dissolved. Remove from the heat and whisk the mixture for 4–5 minutes, or until it holds stiff peaks. Add the maple syrup and maple extract and whisk until combined. Spoon the frosting into a piping bag fitted with a star-shaped tip and pipe onto the cupcakes. Break the reserved candied bacon into 12 pieces and place on top of the cupcakes.

PINK LEMONADE CUPCAKES

Makes: 10

Prep: 35 mins, plus cooling

Cook: 15–20 mins

Ingredients

115 g/4 oz self-raising flour

¼ tsp baking powder

115 g/4 oz butter, softened, or soft margarine

115 g/4 oz caster sugar

2 large eggs

pink food colouring

55 g/2 oz granulated sugar

juice of 1 small lemon

Frosting

115 g/4 oz butter, softened

juice and finely grated rind of ½ lemon

4 tbsp double cream

225 g/8 oz icing sugar

pink food colouring

To decorate

pink and white sugar sprinkles

pink, white and red hundreds and thousands

10 pink or yellow drinking straws

Method

1 Preheat the oven to 180°C/350°F/Gas Mark 4. Line a bun tin with 10 paper cases.

2 Sift the flour and baking powder into a large bowl. Add the butter, caster sugar and eggs and, using an electric hand-held mixer, beat together until just smooth. Beat in a little pink food colouring to colour the mixture pale pink.

3 Spoon the mixture evenly into the paper cases. Bake in the preheated oven for 15–20 minutes, or until well risen, golden and firm to the touch.

4 Meanwhile, place the granulated sugar and lemon juice in a small saucepan and heat gently, stirring, until the sugar has dissolved. Leave to cool for 15 minutes. Prick the tops of the warm cupcakes all over with a skewer and liberally brush with the lemon syrup. Transfer to a wire rack and leave to cool.

5 To make the frosting, place the butter, lemon juice and lemon rind in a bowl and beat with an electric hand-held mixer for 2–3 minutes, or until pale and creamy. Beat in the cream, then gradually sift in the icing sugar and continue beating for 2–3 minutes, or until the frosting is light and fluffy. Beat in a little pink food colouring to give a pale pink colour.

FUN FLAVOUR CUPCAKES

6 Using a small palette knife, thickly swirl the frosting over the tops of the cupcakes. Scatter sugar sprinkles in the centre of five of the cupcakes and edge the remaining cupcakes with hundreds and thousands. Cut the straws to 8-cm/3¼ inch lengths and push into the cupcakes.

CUPCAKE SHOOTERS

Makes: 16

Prep: 30 mins, plus cooling

Cook: 20 mins

Ingredients

150 g/5½ oz self-raising flour
55 g/2 oz ground almonds
175 g/6 oz butter, softened
175 g/6 oz caster sugar
1 tsp vanilla extract
3 eggs, lightly beaten

Frosting

225 g/8 oz butter, softened
about 175 g/6 oz icing sugar (see method)
1 tbsp double cream

Method

1 Preheat the oven to 180°C/350°F/Gas Mark 4. Line two bun tins with 16 paper cases.

2 Sift the flour into a bowl and add the ground almonds. Put the butter and caster sugar into a separate bowl and beat until light and fluffy. Add the vanilla extract, then add the eggs, a little at a time, beating after each addition. Add half of the flour mixture and beat until incorporated. Add the remaining flour mixture and mix.

3 Spoon the mixture evenly into the paper cases. Bake in the preheated oven for 20 minutes, or until well risen, golden and firm to the touch. Transfer to a wire rack and leave to cool.

4 To make the frosting, put the butter, icing sugar and cream into a bowl and beat with an electric hand-held mixer until well combined. Add more icing sugar, if necessary, to achieve a piping consistency. Transfer the frosting to a piping bag fitted with a small star-shaped tip.

5 Crumble the cooled cupcakes into a bowl. Transfer to 16 clear shot glasses, filling each three-quarters full. Pipe the frosting onto the cake crumbs and serve.

EARL GREY CUPCAKES

Makes: 10

Prep: 20 mins, plus cooling

Cook: 20–25 mins

Ingredients

175 g/6 oz plain flour

1 tbsp baking powder

½ tsp ground mixed spice

175 g/6 oz butter, softened, plus extra for greasing

175 g/6 oz golden caster sugar

3 eggs

1 tsp vanilla extract

2 tbsp strong Earl Grey tea

55 g/2 oz currants

icing sugar and mixed spice, for dusting

Method

1 Preheat the oven to 180°C/350°F/Gas Mark 4. Grease ten 200-ml/7-fl oz ovenproof teacups with butter and place on two baking trays.

2 Sift the flour, baking powder and mixed spice into a large bowl and add the butter, caster sugar, eggs and vanilla extract. Beat well with an electric hand-held mixer until just smooth, then stir in the tea and half the currants.

3 Spoon the mixture evenly into the cups and sprinkle with the remaining currants. Bake in the preheated oven for 20–25 minutes, or until well risen, golden and firm to the touch. Transfer to a wire rack and leave to cool.

4 Dust the cupcakes with a little icing sugar and mixed spice before serving.

FUN FLAVOUR CUPCAKES

BLACK FOREST CUPCAKES

Makes: 12

Prep: 30 mins, plus standing & cooling

Cook: 25–30 mins

Ingredients

85 g/3 oz plain chocolate

1 tsp lemon juice

4 tbsp milk

150 g/5½ oz self-raising flour

1 tbsp cocoa powder

½ tsp bicarbonate of soda

2 eggs

55 g/2 oz butter, softened

115 g/4 oz soft light brown sugar

25 g/1 oz dried and sweetened sour cherries, chopped

2 tbsp cherry liqueur (optional)

150 ml/5 fl oz double cream, softly whipped

5 tbsp cherry jam

cocoa powder, to dust

Method

1 Preheat the oven to 180°C/350°F/Gas Mark 4. Line a 12-cup muffin tin with paper cases.

2 Break the chocolate into a heatproof bowl and set the bowl over a saucepan of gently simmering water until melted. Add the lemon juice to the milk and leave for 10 minutes – the milk will curdle a little.

3 Sift the flour, cocoa powder and bicarbonate of soda into a bowl. Add the eggs, butter, sugar and milk mixture and beat with an electric hand-held mixer until just smooth. Fold in the melted chocolate and cherries.

4 Spoon the mixture evenly into the paper cases. Bake in the preheated oven for 20–25 minutes, or until well risen and firm to the touch. Transfer to a wire rack and leave to cool.

5 When the cupcakes are cool, use a serrated knife to cut a circle from the top of each cupcake. Sprinkle the cakes with a little cherry liqueur, if using. Spoon the whipped cream onto the centres and top with a small spoonful of jam. Gently replace the cupcake tops and dust lightly with cocoa powder. Store in the refrigerator until ready to serve.

FUN FLAVOUR CUPCAKES

TIRAMISÙ CUPCAKES

Makes: 12

Prep: 25 mins, plus cooling

Cook: 20–25 mins

Ingredients

115 g/4 oz butter, softened

115 g/4 oz soft light brown sugar

2 eggs

115 g/4 oz self-raising flour

½ tsp baking powder

2 tsp coffee granules

25 g/1 oz icing sugar

4 tbsp water

2 tbsp finely grated plain chocolate, for dusting

Frosting

225 g/8 oz mascarpone cheese

85 g/3 oz caster sugar

2 tbsp Marsala or sweet sherry

Method

1 Preheat the oven to 180°C/350°F/Gas Mark 4. Line a 12-cup bun tin with paper cases.

2 Place the butter, brown sugar, eggs, flour and baking powder in a large bowl and beat together with an electric hand-held mixer until just smooth.

3 Spoon the mixture evenly into the paper cases. Bake in the preheated oven for 15–20 minutes, or until well risen, golden and firm to the touch.

4 Place the coffee granules, icing sugar and water in a saucepan and heat gently, stirring, until the coffee and sugar have dissolved. Boil for 1 minute then leave to cool for 10 minutes. Brush the coffee syrup over the top of the warm cupcakes. Transfer the cupcakes to a wire rack and leave to cool.

5 For the frosting, put the mascarpone, sugar and Marsala in a bowl and beat together until smooth. Spread over the top of the cakes. Using a star template, sprinkle the grated chocolate over the frosting.

PINK MERINGUE CUPCAKES

Makes: 12

Prep: 30 mins, plus cooling & chilling

Cook: 25 mins

Ingredients

200 g/7 oz plain flour

1½ tsp baking powder

¼ tsp salt

115 g/4 oz butter, softened

200 g/7 oz caster sugar

1 tsp vanilla extract

2 large eggs, lightly beaten

finely grated rind and juice of 1 lemon

4 tbsp milk

pink food colouring

Filling

225 ml/8 oz lemon curd

125 ml/4 fl oz double cream, whipped

Frosting

4 large egg whites

200 g/7 oz granulated sugar

¼ tsp cream of tartar

1 tbsp lemon juice

1 tsp lemon extract

pink food colouring

Method

1 Preheat the oven to 180°C/350°F/Gas Mark 4. Line a 12-cup bun tin with paper cases.

2 Sift together the flour, baking powder and salt in a bowl. Put the butter and caster sugar into a separate bowl and beat until light and fluffy. Add the vanilla extract, then add the eggs, a little at a time, beating after each addition. Add half of the flour mixture, the lemon rind and juice and the milk, and beat until combined. Add the remaining flour mixture and mix. Add a few drops of food colouring and stir until evenly incorporated.

3 Spoon the mixture evenly into the paper cases. Bake in the preheated oven for 20 minutes, or until well risen, golden and firm to the touch. Transfer to a wire rack and leave to cool.

4 To make the filling, gently fold the lemon curd into the whipped cream and chill until ready to use.

5 Use an apple corer to remove the centre of each cupcake. Spoon the lemon curd filling into the holes.

6 To make the frosting, put the egg whites, granulated sugar and cream of tartar in a heatproof bowl set over a saucepan of gently simmering water and whisk until the sugar has

FUN FLAVOUR CUPCAKES

completely dissolved. Remove from the heat and whisk the mixture for 4–5 minutes, or until it holds stiff peaks. Add the lemon juice, lemon extract and a few drops of food colouring and beat until combined.

7 Spoon the frosting into a piping bag fitted with a large round tip and pipe onto the cupcakes.

POMEGRANATE & GREEN TEA CUPCAKES

Makes: 12 **Prep: 30 mins,** plus cooling **Cook: 35 mins**

Ingredients

190 g/6¾ oz plain flour

1½ tsp baking powder

1 tbsp green tea powder

½ tsp salt

115 g/4 oz butter, softened

200 g/7 oz caster sugar

1 tsp vanilla extract

2 large eggs, lightly beaten

4 tbsp milk

pomegranate seeds,
to decorate

Pomegranate syrup

475 ml/17 fl oz
pomegranate juice

100 g/3½ oz caster sugar

Frosting

115 g/4 oz butter, softened

about 300 g/10½ oz icing
sugar (see method)

Method

1 To make the pomegranate syrup, put the pomegranate juice and the sugar into a saucepan and bring to the boil over a medium–high heat, stirring occasionally, until the sugar has dissolved. Reduce the heat to low and cook until the mixture has reduced to about 125 ml/4 fl oz. Set aside to cool.

2 Preheat the oven to 180°C/350°F/Gas Mark 4. Line a 12-cup bun tin with paper cases.

3 Sift together the flour, baking powder, green tea powder and salt into a bowl. Put the butter and caster sugar into a separate bowl and beat until light and fluffy. Add the vanilla extract, then add the eggs, a little at a time, beating after each addition. Add half of the flour mixture, 4 tablespoons of the pomegranate syrup and the milk and mix to incorporate. Add the remaining flour mixture and mix.

4 Spoon the mixture evenly into the paper cases. Bake in the preheated oven for 20 minutes, or until well risen, golden and firm to the touch. Transfer to a wire rack and leave to cool.

5 To make the frosting, put the butter, icing sugar and remaining pomegranate syrup in a bowl and beat with an electric hand-held mixer until well combined. Add more icing sugar, if

FUN FLAVOUR CUPCAKES

necessary, to achieve a piping consistency. Spoon the frosting into a piping bag fitted with a star-shaped tip and pipe onto the cupcakes.

6 To decorate, sprinkle the pomegranate seeds over the cupcakes.

SECRET BISCUIT CUPCAKES

Makes: 12

Prep: 35 mins, plus cooling

Cook: 20 mins

Ingredients

12 chocolate sandwich biscuits

125 g/4½ oz plain flour

60 g/2¼ oz cocoa powder

1½ tsp baking powder

¼ tsp salt

55 g/2 oz butter, softened

200 g/7 oz caster sugar

2 tsp vanilla extract

2 large eggs, lightly beaten

125 ml/4 fl oz double cream

12 mini chocolate sandwich biscuits, to decorate

Frosting

225 g/8 oz butter, softened

about 175 g/6 oz icing sugar (see method)

2 tbsp milk

1 tsp vanilla extract

pinch of salt

6 chocolate sandwich biscuits

Method

1 Preheat the oven to 180°C/350°F/Gas Mark 4. Line a 12-cup bun tin with paper cases. Place a biscuit in the base of each case.

2 Sift together the flour, cocoa powder, baking powder and salt in a bowl. Put the butter and caster sugar into a separate bowl and beat until light and fluffy. Add the vanilla extract, then add the eggs, a little at a time, beating after each addition. Add half of the flour mixture and the cream and beat until incorporated. Add the remaining flour mixture and mix.

3 Spoon the mixture evenly into the paper cases over the biscuits. Bake in the preheated oven for 20 minutes, or until well risen and firm to the touch. Transfer to a wire rack and leave to cool.

4 To make the frosting, put the butter into a bowl and beat with an electric hand-held mixer until creamy. Add the icing sugar, milk, vanilla extract and salt. Separate the 6 sandwich biscuits and scrape the cream filling into the frosting, reserving the biscuits. Beat together until well combined. Add more icing sugar, if necessary, to achieve a piping consistency.

5 In a food processor, coarsely grind the reserved biscuits. Add to the frosting and mix until just combined. Spoon the frosting into a piping bag fitted with a star-shaped tip and pipe onto the cupcakes.

6 Decorate each cupcake with one of the mini biscuits and serve.

VEGAN ALMOND CUPCAKES

Makes: 10

Prep: 25 mins, plus cooling

Cook: 25–30 mins

Ingredients

5 tbsp rapeseed oil

4 tbsp plain soya yogurt

160 ml/5½ fl oz soya milk

160 g/5¾ oz caster sugar

3 tbsp almond extract

40 g/1½ oz ground almonds

160 g/5¾ oz plain flour

1½ tsp baking powder

½ tsp salt

toasted flaked almonds, to decorate

Frosting

60 g/2¼ oz vegan white or milk chocolate

100 g/3½ oz icing sugar

1½ tbsp soya milk

Method

1 Preheat the oven to 180°C/350°F/Gas Mark 4. Line a bun tin with 10 paper cases.

2 Place the oil, yogurt, milk, sugar, almond extract and ground almonds in a large mixing bowl. Sift in the flour, baking powder and salt then beat with an electric hand-held mixer until the mixture is well combined.

3 Spoon the mixture evenly into the paper cases. Bake in the preheated oven for 20–25 minutes, or until well risen, golden and firm to the touch. Transfer to a wire rack and leave to cool.

4 To make the frosting, melt the chocolate in a large heatproof bowl set over a pan of simmering water. Remove from the heat and leave to cool slightly. Beat in the icing sugar and soya milk and spread the frosting over the cupcakes with a teaspoon while the frosting is still a little warm and easy to spread. Top each cupcake with a few toasted flaked almonds.

FUN FLAVOUR CUPCAKES

HOT MARMALADE
CUPCAKES

Makes: 4   **Prep: 20 mins,**   **Cook: 1½ hrs**
plus cooling

Ingredients

1 small orange

85 g/3 oz butter, softened,
plus extra for greasing

85 g/3 oz caster sugar

1 large egg

115 g/4 oz self-raising flour

2 tbsp fine shred
marmalade, warmed

crème fraîche, to serve

Method

1 Put the orange in a saucepan and cover with
water. Bring to the boil then reduce the heat and
cover and simmer for 1 hour until soft. Remove
the orange from the water and leave to cool for
30 minutes.

2 Preheat the oven to 180°C/350°F/Gas Mark 4.
Grease four 150-ml/5-fl oz ovenproof teacups or
dishes (such as ramekins).

3 Cut the orange into chunks and remove any
pips. Put all the orange chunks (rind included)
into a food processor and blend until finely
minced. Add the butter, sugar, egg and flour and
process until well blended.

4 Spoon the mixture evenly into the teacups. Put
the cups on a baking sheet and bake in the
preheated oven for 25–30 minutes, or until well
risen, golden and firm to the touch. Cool for
2–3 minutes then brush the warmed marmalade
over the top of each cupcake. Serve with
crème fraîche.

FUN FLAVOUR CUPCAKES

BUTTERSCOTCH CUPCAKES

Makes: 28

Prep: 25 mins, plus cooling

Cook: 20–25 mins

Ingredients

175 g/6 oz plain flour

1 tbsp baking powder

175 g/6 oz butter, softened

175 g/6 oz light muscovado sugar

3 eggs

1 tsp vanilla extract

Topping

2 tbsp golden syrup

25 g/1 oz butter

2 tbsp light muscovado sugar

Method

1 Preheat the oven to 190°C/375°F/Gas Mark 5. Line three bun tins with 28 paper cases.

2 Sift the flour and baking powder into a large bowl and add the butter, sugar, eggs and vanilla extract. Beat well with an electric hand-held mixer until the mixture is just smooth.

3 Spoon the mixture evenly into the paper cases. Bake in the preheated oven for 15–20 minutes, or until well risen, golden and firm to the touch. Transfer to a wire rack and leave to cool.

4 To make the topping, place the golden syrup, butter and sugar in a small pan and heat gently, stirring, until the sugar dissolves. Bring to the boil and cook, stirring, for about 1 minute. Drizzle over the cupcakes and leave to set.

FUN FLAVOUR CUPCAKES

DOUBLE GINGER CUPCAKES

Makes: 12

Prep: 25 mins, plus cooling

Cook: 15–20 mins

Ingredients

175 g/6 oz plain flour

1 tbsp baking powder

2 tsp ground ginger

175 g/6 oz butter, softened

175 g/6 oz light muscovado sugar

3 eggs

25 g/1 oz crystallized stem ginger, finely chopped

diced crystallized stem ginger, to decorate

Frosting

200 g/7 oz ricotta cheese

85 g/3 oz icing sugar, sifted

finely grated rind of 1 tangerine

Method

1 Preheat the oven to 190°C/375°F/Gas Mark 5. Line a 12-cup bun tin with paper cases.

2 Sift the flour, baking powder and ground ginger into a large bowl. Add the butter, muscovado sugar and eggs and beat well with an electric hand-held mixer until just smooth. Stir in the crystallized ginger.

3 Spoon the mixture evenly into the paper cases. Bake in the preheated oven for 15–20 minutes, or until well risen, golden and firm to the touch. Transfer to a wire rack and leave to cool.

4 To make the frosting, mix together the ricotta, icing sugar and tangerine rind until smooth. Spoon a little frosting onto each cake and spread over the surface to cover.

5 Top the cupcakes with diced crystallized ginger and serve.

FUN FLAVOUR CUPCAKES

LIMONCELLO CUPCAKES

Makes: 12

Prep: 30 mins, plus cooling

Cook: 25 mins

Ingredients

190 g/6¾ oz plain flour

1½ tsp baking powder

¼ tsp salt

115 g/4 oz butter, softened

200 g/7 oz caster sugar

2 large eggs, lightly beaten

finely grated rind and juice of 1 lemon

4 tbsp milk

hundreds and thousands, to decorate

Frosting

3 large egg whites

150 g/5½ oz granulated sugar

225 g/8 oz butter, softened

4 tbsp limoncello

finely grated rind of 1 lemon

Method

1 Preheat the oven to 180°C/350°F/Gas Mark 4. Line a 12-cup bun tin with paper cases.

2 Sift together the flour, baking powder and salt in a bowl. Put the butter and caster sugar into a separate bowl and beat until light and fluffy. Add the eggs, a little at a time, beating after each addition. Add half of the flour mixture, the lemon rind and juice and the milk and beat. Add the remaining flour mixture and mix.

3 Spoon the mixture evenly into the paper cases. Bake in the preheated oven for 20 minutes, or until well risen, golden and firm to the touch. Transfer to a wire rack and leave to cool.

4 To make the frosting, put the egg whites and granulated sugar in a heatproof bowl set over a saucepan of gently simmering water and whisk until the sugar has completely dissolved. Remove from the heat and whisk the mixture for 4–5 minutes. Add the butter, 2 tablespoons at a time, and continue to beat until it holds stiff peaks. Add the limoncello and lemon rind and beat until just combined.

5 Spoon the frosting into a piping bag fitted with a star-shaped tip and pipe onto the cupcakes. Sprinkle with hundreds and thousands.

FUN FLAVOUR CUPCAKES

CHOCOLATE & DARK ALE CUPCAKES

Makes: 12

Prep: 40 mins, plus cooling

Cook: 25 mins

Ingredients

125 g/4½ oz plain flour

60 g/2¼ oz cocoa powder

1½ tsp baking powder

¼ tsp salt

115 g/4 oz butter, softened

200 g/7 oz caster sugar

1 tsp vanilla extract

2 large eggs, lightly beaten

125 ml/4 fl oz dark ale

Frosting

3 large egg whites

160 g/5¾ oz soft light brown sugar

160 g/5¾ oz butter, softened

1½ tsp vanilla extract

To decorate

55 g/2 oz green ready-to-roll fondant icing

icing sugar, for dusting

yellow sugar crystals

Method

1 Preheat the oven to 180°C/350°F/Gas Mark 4. Line a 12-cup bun tin with paper cases.

2 Sift together the flour, cocoa powder, baking powder and salt into a bowl. Put the butter and caster sugar into a separate bowl and beat with an electric hand-held mixer until light and fluffy. Add the vanilla extract, then add the eggs, a little at a time, beating after each addition. Add half of the flour mixture and the ale, and beat until incorporated. Add the remaining flour mixture and mix.

3 Spoon the mixture evenly into the paper cases. Bake in the preheated oven for 20 minutes, or until well risen and firm to the touch. Transfer to a wire rack and leave to cool.

4 To make the frosting, put the egg whites and brown sugar in a heatproof bowl set over a saucepan of gently simmering water and whisk until the sugar has completely dissolved. Remove from the heat and whisk the mixture for 4–5 minutes. Add the butter, 2 tablespoons at a time, and continue to whisk until it holds stiff peaks. Add the vanilla extract and beat until just

combined. Spoon the frosting into a piping bag fitted with a star-shaped tip and pipe onto the cupcakes.

5 To make the clover decorations, roll out the fondant icing on a work surface lightly dusted with icing sugar until it is 5 mm/¼ inch thick. Cut out 12 clover shapes and set aside to dry.

6 Place a clover leaf on top of each cupcake and sprinkle with yellow sugar crystals.

CHILLI CHOCOLATE CUPCAKES

Makes: 12

Prep: 25 mins, plus cooling

Cook: 20 mins

Ingredients

125 g/4½ oz plain flour

75 g/2¾ oz cocoa powder

1½ tsp baking powder

½ tsp ground cinnamon

1 tsp mild chilli powder

¼ tsp cayenne pepper

¼ tsp salt

115 g/4 oz butter, softened

200 g/7 oz caster sugar

2 tsp vanilla extract

2 large eggs, lightly beaten

125 ml/4 fl oz milk

2 squares plain chocolate, grated, to decorate

Frosting

115 g/4 oz butter, softened

about 190 g/6¾ oz icing sugar (see method)

40 g/1½ oz cocoa powder

2 tbsp milk

1 tsp vanilla extract

1 tsp ground cinnamon

Method

1 Preheat the oven to 180°C/350°F/Gas Mark 4. Line a 12-cup bun tin with paper cases.

2 Sift together the flour, cocoa powder, baking powder, cinnamon, chilli powder, cayenne pepper and salt into a bowl. Put the butter and caster sugar into a separate bowl and beat until light and fluffy. Add the vanilla extract, then add the eggs, a little at a time, beating after each addition. Add half of the flour mixture and the milk and beat until incorporated. Add the remaining flour mixture and mix.

3 Spoon the mixture evenly into the paper cases. Bake in the preheated oven for 20 minutes, or until well risen and firm to the touch. Transfer to a wire rack and leave to cool.

4 To make the frosting, put the butter in a bowl and beat with an electric hand-held mixer until light and fluffy. Add the icing sugar together with the cocoa powder, milk, vanilla extract and cinnamon. Beat together until well combined. Add more icing sugar, if necessary, to achieve a piping consistency. Spoon the frosting into a piping bag fitted with a star-shaped tip and pipe onto the cupcakes. To decorate, sprinkle the grated chocolate over the top of the cupcakes.

GLUTEN-FREE CARROT CUPCAKES

Makes: 9

Prep: 25 mins, plus cooling

Cook: 18–20 mins

Ingredients

115 g/4 oz light soft brown sugar

90 ml/6 tbsp sunflower oil

2 eggs, lightly beaten

a pinch of saffron strands, crumbled

115 g/4 oz gluten-free self-raising flour, sifted

½ tsp gluten-free baking powder

1 tsp xanthan gum

½ tsp mixed spice

235 g/8½ oz grated carrot

50 g/1¾ oz chopped walnuts

flaked almonds, to decorate

Frosting

100 g/3½ oz gluten-free soft cheese

40 g/1½ oz butter, softened

10 g/¼ oz ground almonds

zest of 2 limes

250 g/9 oz gluten-free icing sugar

Method

1 Preheat the oven to 180°C/350°F/Gas Mark 4. Line a muffin tin with 9 paper cases.

2 Beat together the sugar, oil, eggs and saffron in a large bowl until creamy. Then add the sifted flour, baking powder, xanthan gum, mixed spice, grated carrot and chopped walnuts and mix gently together.

3 Spoon the mixture evenly into the paper cases. Bake in the preheated oven for 18–20 minutes, or until well risen, golden and firm to the touch. Transfer to a wire rack and leave to cool.

4 To make the frosting, process the soft cheese, butter, ground almonds, lime zest and icing sugar until fluffy in a food processor.

5 Place the frosting in a piping bag and decorate each cupcake with swirls of frosting when completely cool. Finish by sprinkling over the flaked almonds.

ORANGE & POPPY SEED CUPCAKES

Makes: 12

Prep: 25 mins,
plus standing & cooling

Cook: 25 mins

Ingredients

2 tbsp poppy seeds,
plus extra to decorate

2 tbsp hot milk

85 g/3 oz butter, softened

85 g/3 oz caster sugar

finely grated rind of
½ orange

1 large egg, lightly beaten

100 g/3½ oz self-raising flour

Frosting

85 g/3 oz butter, softened

finely grated rind of
½ orange

175 g/6 oz icing sugar, sifted

1–2 tbsp orange juice

Method

1 Preheat the oven to 180°C/350°F/Gas Mark 4. Line a 12-cup bun tin with paper cases. Place the poppy seeds and milk in a small bowl and set aside for 10 minutes.

2 Put the butter, sugar and orange rind in a bowl and beat together until light and fluffy. Gradually beat in the egg. Sift in the flour and, using a metal spoon, fold gently into the mixture with the poppy seeds and milk.

3 Spoon the mixture evenly into the paper cases. Bake in the preheated oven for 20 minutes, or until well risen, golden and firm to the touch. Transfer to a wire rack and leave to cool.

4 To make the frosting, put the butter and orange rind in a bowl and beat until fluffy. Gradually beat in the icing sugar and enough orange juice to make a smooth and creamy frosting. Put the frosting in a piping bag, fitted with a large star nozzle. When the cupcakes are cool, pipe a swirl on top of each cupcake and decorate with the poppy seeds.

PEAR & CHOCOLATE CUPCAKES

Makes: 12

Prep: 25 mins,
plus cooling

Cook: 25 mins

Ingredients

115 g/4 oz soft margarine

115 g/4 oz light soft brown sugar

2 eggs

100 g/3½ oz self-raising flour

½ tsp baking powder

2 tbsp cocoa powder

4 canned pear halves, drained and sliced

2 tbsp runny honey, warmed

Method

1 Preheat the oven to 190°C/375°F/Gas Mark 5. Line a 12-cup bun tin with paper cases.

2 Put the margarine, sugar, eggs, flour, baking powder and cocoa powder in a large bowl and, using an electric hand-held mixer, beat together until just smooth.

3 Spoon the mixture evenly into the paper cases. Arrange two pear slices on top of each cupcake. Bake in the preheated oven for 20 minutes, or until well risen and firm to the touch. Transfer to a wire rack.

4 Whilst the cupcakes are still warm, glaze with the honey. Leave to cool completely.

QUEEN CUPCAKES

Makes: 18

Prep: 15 mins, plus cooling

Cook: 15–20 mins

Ingredients

115 g/4 oz butter, softened
115 g/4 oz caster sugar
2 large eggs, lightly beaten
4 tsp lemon juice
175 g/6 oz self-raising flour
115 g/4 oz currants
2–4 tbsp milk, if necessary

Method

1 Preheat the oven to 190°C/375°F/Gas Mark 5. Line two bun tins with 18 paper cases.

2 Put the butter and sugar in a bowl and beat together until light and fluffy. Gradually beat in the eggs, then beat in the lemon juice with 1 tablespoon of the flour. Sift in the remaining flour, then fold in gently with the currants, using a metal spoon. Add a little milk, if necessary, to give a soft dropping consistency.

3 Spoon the mixture evenly into the paper cases. Bake in the preheated oven for 15–20 minutes, or until well risen, golden and firm to the touch. Transfer to a wire rack and leave to cool.

CHERRY BAKEWELL CUPCAKES

Makes: 4

Prep: 20 mins,
plus cooling & setting

Cook: 25–30 mins

Ingredients

55 g/2 oz butter, softened, plus extra for greasing

55 g/2 oz caster sugar

1 large egg, lightly beaten

55 g/2 oz self-raising flour

40 g/1½ oz ground almonds

½ tsp almond extract

1 tbsp milk

40 g/1½ oz glacé cherries, quartered

1 tbsp toasted flaked almonds, to decorate

Topping

40 g/1½ oz icing sugar

2 tsp lemon juice

Method

1 Preheat the oven to 180°C/350°F/Gas Mark 4. Grease four 200-ml/7-fl oz ovenproof teacups or dishes (such as ramekins).

2 Put the butter and sugar in a bowl and beat together until light and fluffy. Gradually beat in the egg. Sift in the flour and, using a metal spoon, fold into the mixture with the ground almonds, almond extract and milk.

3 Spoon the mixture evenly into the teacups. Scatter over the cherries. Put the cups on a baking sheet and bake in the preheated oven for 25–30 minutes, or until well risen, golden and firm to the touch.

4 To make the topping, sift the icing sugar into a bowl and stir in the lemon juice to make a smooth mixture. Using a teaspoon, drizzle the topping over the cupcakes and decorate with flaked almonds. Leave to set.

FUN FLAVOUR CUPCAKES

CHOCOLATE BROWNIE CUPCAKES

Makes: 12

Prep: 20 mins, plus cooling

Cook: 35 mins

Ingredients

225 g/8 oz plain chocolate, broken into pieces

85 g/3 oz butter

2 large eggs, lightly beaten

200 g/7 oz soft dark brown sugar

1 tsp vanilla extract

140 g/5 oz plain flour

75g/2¾ oz walnuts, chopped into small pieces

Method

1 Preheat the oven to 180°C/350°F/Gas Mark 4. Line a 12-cup muffin tin with paper cases.

2 Place the chocolate and butter in a saucepan and heat gently, stirring constantly, until melted. Remove from the heat and stir until smooth. Leave to cool slightly.

3 Place the eggs and sugar in a large bowl and whisk together, then add the vanilla extract. Sift in the flour and stir until combined, then stir the melted chocolate into the mixture until combined. Stir in the chopped walnuts.

4 Spoon the mixture evenly into the paper cases. Bake in the preheated oven for 30 minutes, or until firm to the touch but still slightly moist in the centre. Transfer to a wire rack and leave to cool.

FUN FLAVOUR CUPCAKES

FEATHER-ICED COFFEE CUPCAKES

Makes: 16

Prep: 30 mins, plus cooling

Cook: 20 mins

Ingredients

115 g/4 oz butter, softened

115 g/4 oz soft light brown sugar

2 eggs

115 g/4 oz self-raising flour

½ tsp baking powder

1 tbsp instant coffee granules dissolved in 1 tbsp boiling water

2 tbsp soured cream

Frosting

225 g/8 oz icing sugar

4 tsp warm water

1 tbsp instant coffee granules dissolved in 2 tbsp boiling water

Method

1 Preheat the oven to 190°C/375°F/Gas Mark 5. Line two bun tins with 16 paper cases.

2 Put the butter, sugar and eggs in a bowl. Sift in the flour and baking powder, then beat together with an electric hand-held mixer until just smooth. Add the dissolved coffee and soured cream and beat together until well mixed.

3 Spoon the mixture evenly into the paper cases. Bake in the preheated oven for 20 minutes, or until well risen, golden and firm to the touch. Transfer to a wire rack and leave to cool.

4 To make the frosting, sift 140 g/5 oz of the icing sugar into a bowl, then gradually mix in the water. Sift the remaining icing sugar into a bowl, then stir in the dissolved coffee. Put the coffee icing in a piping bag, fitted with a piping nozzle. When the cupcakes are cool, coat the tops of the cupcakes with the white frosting and pipe the coffee frosting across in parallel lines. Draw a skewer across the piped lines in both directions.

GLUTEN-FREE CHOCOLATE & NUT CUPCAKES

Makes: 12　　　**Prep: 20 mins,**　　　**Cook: 25–30 mins**
　　　　　　　　　　plus cooling

Ingredients

200 g/7 oz caster sugar

½ tsp glycerine

190 g/6½ oz butter, softened

4 eggs, lightly beaten

55 g/2 oz gluten-free cocoa powder

175 g/6 oz gluten-free self-raising flour

¼ tsp gluten-free baking powder

¼ tsp xanthan gum

70 g/2½ oz macadamia nuts, chopped

Method

1 Preheat the oven to 180°C/350°F/Gas Mark 4. Line a 12-cup muffin tin with paper cases.

2 Put the sugar, glycerine and butter in a bowl and beat together until light and fluffy. Gradually beat in the eggs, a little at a time. Beat well after each addition.

3 Sift the cocoa powder, flour, baking powder and xanthan gum into the mixture and fold in gently. Carefully fold in half of the macadamia nuts with 3 tablespoons of warm water.

4 Spoon the mixture evenly into the paper cases. Sprinkle with the remaining nuts.

5 Bake in the preheated oven for 25-30 minutes, or until the nuts are golden and the cupcakes are well risen and firm to the touch. Transfer to a wire rack and leave to cool.

CARAMEL CUPCAKES

Makes: 12

Prep: 20 mins, plus cooling

Cook: 20–25 mins

Ingredients

85 g/3 oz butter, softened

55 g/2 oz soft dark brown sugar

1 tbsp golden syrup

1 large egg, lightly beaten

100 g/3½ oz self-raising flour

1 tsp grated nutmeg

2 tbsp milk

Frosting

115 g/4 oz soft light brown sugar

1 small egg white

1 tbsp hot water

pinch of cream of tartar

Method

1 Preheat the oven to 180°C/350°F/Gas Mark 4. Line a 12-cup bun tin with paper cases.

2 Put the butter, sugar and golden syrup in a bowl and beat together until light and fluffy. Gradually beat in the egg. Sift in the flour and, using a metal spoon, fold gently into the mixture with the nutmeg and milk.

3 Spoon the mixture evenly into the paper cases. Bake in the preheated oven for 15–20 minutes, or until well risen, golden and firm to the touch. Transfer to a wire rack and leave to cool.

4 To make the frosting, put all the ingredients in a heatproof bowl set over a saucepan of simmering water. Using an electric hand-held mixer, beat for 5–6 minutes, or until the mixture is thick and softly peaking when the whisk is lifted. Swirl the frosting over the cupcakes.

ROCKY ROAD CUPCAKES

Makes: 12

Prep: 25 mins, plus cooling & setting

Cook: 25 mins

Ingredients

2 tbsp cocoa powder

2 tbsp hot water

115 g/4 oz butter, softened

115 g/4 oz caster sugar

2 eggs, lightly beaten

115 g/4 oz self-raising flour

Topping

25 g/1 oz chopped mixed nuts

100 g/3½ oz milk chocolate, melted

115 g/4 oz mini marshmallows

40 g/1½ oz glacé cherries, chopped

Method

1 Preheat the oven to 180°C/350°F/Gas Mark 4. Line a 12-cup muffin tin with paper cases.

2 Blend the cocoa powder and hot water together and set aside. Put the butter and sugar in a bowl and beat together until light and fluffy. Gradually beat in the eggs then beat in the blended cocoa. Sift in the flour and, using a metal spoon, fold gently into the mixture.

3 Spoon the mixture evenly into the paper cases. Bake in the preheated oven for 20 minutes, or until well risen and firm to the touch. Transfer to a wire rack and leave to cool.

4 To make the topping, stir the nuts into the melted chocolate and spread a little of the mixture over the top of the cakes. Lightly stir the marshmallows and cherries into the remaining chocolate mixture and pile on top of the cupcakes. Leave to set.

★ **Variation**

You could also make the topping with raisins or sultanas instead of marshmallows, if you prefer a more fruity topping.

EVERYDAY MUFFINS

CRANBERRY MUFFINS

Makes: 10

Prep: 20 mins, plus cooling

Cook: 20 mins

Ingredients

175 g/6 oz self-raising flour

55 g/2 oz self-raising wholemeal flour

1 tsp ground cinnamon

½ tsp bicarbonate of soda

1 egg

70 g/2½ oz fine-cut marmalade

150 ml/5 fl oz skimmed or semi-skimmed milk

5 tbsp corn oil, plus extra for greasing

115 g/4 oz eating apple, peeled and finely diced

115 g/4 oz fresh or frozen cranberries, thawed if frozen

1 tbsp rolled oats

Method

1 Preheat the oven to 200°C/400°F/Gas Mark 6. Grease a 10-cup muffin tin or line with 10 paper cases. Sift together the flours, cinnamon and bicarbonate of soda into a large bowl, adding any husks that remain in the sieve.

2 Lightly beat the egg with the marmalade in a large jug, then beat in the milk and oil. Make a well in the centre of the dry ingredients and pour in the beaten liquid ingredients. Stir gently until just combined; do not over-mix. Stir in the apple and cranberries.

3 Divide the mixture evenly between the holes in the prepared muffin tin and sprinkle the oats over the tops of the muffins. Bake in the preheated oven for about 20 minutes, or until well risen, golden and firm to the touch.

4 Transfer to a wire rack and leave to cool.

★ **Variation**

For a more summmery cupcake, replace the cranberries with the same amount of blackcurrants.

DARK & WHITE MUFFINS

Makes: 12

Prep: 25 mins,
plus cooling & setting

Cook: 25 mins

Ingredients

200 g/7 oz plain flour

25 g/1 oz cocoa powder

1 tbsp baking powder

1 tsp ground cinnamon

115 g/4 oz caster sugar

185 g/6½ oz white chocolate, chopped

2 eggs

225 ml/8 fl oz milk

100 ml/3½ fl oz sunflower oil, plus extra for greasing

Method

1 Preheat the oven to 200°C/400°F/Gas Mark 6. Grease a 12-cup muffin tin or line with 12 paper cases. Sift together the flour, cocoa powder, baking powder and cinnamon into a large bowl. Stir in the sugar and 125 g/4½ oz of the chocolate.

2 Lightly beat the eggs in a large jug, then beat in the milk and oil. Make a well in the centre of the dry ingredients and pour in the beaten liquid ingredients. Stir gently until just combined; do not over-mix.

3 Divide the mixture evenly between the holes in the prepared muffin tin. Bake in the preheated oven for 20 minutes, or until well risen and firm to the touch.

4 Transfer to a wire rack and leave to cool.

5 Melt the remaining chocolate in a heatproof bowl set over a pan of gently simmering water. Drizzle the melted chocolate over the tops of the muffins. Leave to set.

FUDGE NUT MUFFINS

Makes: 12

Prep: 20 mins, plus cooling

Cook: 25–30 mins

Ingredients

250 g/9 oz plain flour

4 tsp baking powder

85 g/3 oz caster sugar

6 tbsp crunchy peanut butter

1 large egg

175 ml/6 fl oz milk

55 g/2 oz butter, melted, plus extra for greasing

150 g/5½ oz vanilla fudge, cut into small pieces

3 tbsp roughly chopped unsalted peanuts

Method

1 Preheat the oven to 200°C/400°F/Gas Mark 6. Grease a 12-cup muffin tin or line with 12 paper cases. Sift together the flour and baking powder into a large bowl. Stir in the sugar. Add the peanut butter and stir until the mixture resembles breadcrumbs.

2 Lightly beat the egg in a large jug, then beat in the milk and melted butter. Make a well in the centre of the dry ingredients, pour in the beaten liquid ingredients and add the fudge pieces. Stir gently until just combined; do not over-mix.

3 Divide the mixture evenly between the holes in the prepared muffin tin. Sprinkle the peanuts over the tops of the muffins. Bake in the preheated oven for 20–25 minutes, or until well risen, golden and firm to the touch.

4 Transfer to a wire rack and leave to cool.

WHOLEMEAL MUFFINS

Makes: 10

Prep: 25 mins, plus cooling

Cook: 25–30 mins

Ingredients

225 g/8 oz self-raising wholemeal flour

2 tsp baking powder

25 g/1 oz light muscovado sugar

100 g/3½ oz ready-to-eat dried apricots, finely chopped

1 banana, mashed with 1 tbsp orange juice

1 tsp orange rind, finely grated

300 ml/10 fl oz skimmed milk

1 egg, beaten

3 tbsp corn oil, plus extra for greasing

2 tbsp rolled oats

fruit spread, honey or maple syrup, to serve

Method

1 Preheat the oven to 200°C/400°F/Gas Mark 6. Grease a 10-cup muffin tin or line with 10 paper cases. Sift the flour and baking powder into a mixing bowl, adding any husks that remain in the sieve. Stir in the sugar and chopped apricots.

2 Make a well in the centre of the dry ingredients and add the banana, orange rind, milk, beaten egg and oil. Stir gently until just combined; do not over-mix.

3 Divide the mixture evenly between the holes in the prepared muffin tin. Sprinkle each muffin with a few rolled oats and bake in the preheated oven for 25–30 minutes, or until well risen, golden and firm to the touch.

4 Transfer to a wire rack and leave to cool slightly. Serve the muffins warm with a little fruit spread, honey or maple syrup.

CHOCOLATE ORANGE MUFFINS

Makes: 12

Prep: 25 mins, plus cooling

Cook: 25 mins

Ingredients

2 oranges

about 125 ml/4 fl oz milk

225 g/8 oz plain flour

55 g/2 oz cocoa powder

1 tbsp baking powder

pinch of salt

115 g/4 oz soft light brown sugar

150 g/5½ oz plain chocolate chips

2 eggs

6 tbsp sunflower oil or 85 g/3 oz butter, melted, plus extra for greasing

strips of orange zest, to decorate

Frosting

55 g/2 oz plain chocolate, broken into pieces

25 g/1 oz butter

2 tbsp water

175 g/6 oz icing sugar

Method

1 Preheat the oven to 200°C/400°F/Gas Mark 6. Grease a 12-cup muffin tin or line with 12 paper cases. Finely grate the rind from the oranges and squeeze the juice. Add enough milk to make up the juice to 250 ml/9 fl oz, then add the orange rind. Sift together the flour, cocoa, baking powder and salt into a large bowl. Stir in the brown sugar and chocolate chips. Place the eggs in a large jug or bowl and beat lightly, then beat in the milk and orange mixture and the oil. Make a well in the centre of the dry ingredients and pour in the beaten liquid ingredients. Stir gently until just combined; do not over-mix.

2 Divide the mixture evenly between the holes in the prepared muffin tin. Bake in the preheated oven for 20 minutes, or until well risen and firm to the touch. Transfer to a wire rack and leave to cool completely.

3 To make the frosting, place the chocolate in a heatproof bowl, add the butter and water, then set the bowl over a saucepan of gently simmering water and heat, stirring, until melted. Remove from the heat, sift in the icing sugar and beat until smooth, then spread the frosting on top of the muffins and decorate with strips of orange zest.

MOCHA MUFFINS

Makes: 12

Prep: 25 mins,
plus cooling

Cook: 25 mins

Ingredients

225 g/8 oz plain flour
1 tbsp baking powder
2 tbsp cocoa powder
pinch of salt
115 g/4 oz butter, melted,
plus extra for greasing
150 g/5½ oz brown sugar
1 large egg, lightly beaten
125 ml/4 fl oz milk
1 tsp almond extract
3 tbsp strong coffee
55 g/2 oz chocolate chips
25 g/1 oz raisins

Topping

3 tbsp demerara sugar
1 tbsp cocoa powder
1 tsp ground allspice

Method

1 Preheat the oven to 190°C/375°F/Gas Mark 5.
Grease a 12-cup muffin tin or line with 12 paper
cases. To make the topping, place the sugar,
cocoa powder and allspice in a small bowl and
mix together well. Set aside.

2 Sift together the flour, baking powder, cocoa
powder and salt into a large bowl.

3 Place the melted butter and sugar in a
separate large bowl and beat together until
light and fluffy, then stir in the egg. Pour in the
milk, almond extract and coffee, then add
the chocolate chips and raisins and gently
mix together.

4 Make a well in the centre of the dry ingredients
and pour in the liquid ingredients. Stir gently until
just combined; do not over-mix.

5 Divide the mixture evenly between the holes in
the prepared muffin tin and sprinkle the cocoa
topping over the tops of the muffins. Bake in the
preheated oven for 20 minutes, or until well risen
and firm to the touch.

6 Serve warm or transfer to a wire rack and leave
to cool.

EVERYDAY MUFFINS

APPLE STREUSEL MUFFINS

Makes: 12

Prep: 25 mins,
plus cooling

Cook: 25 mins

Ingredients

280 g/10 oz plain flour

1 tbsp baking powder

½ tsp ground cinnamon

pinch of salt

115 g/4 oz soft light brown sugar

1 large cooking apple, peeled and finely chopped

2 eggs

250 ml/9 fl oz milk

85 g/3 oz butter, melted, plus extra for greasing

Topping

50 g/1½ oz plain flour

½ tsp ground cinnamon

35 g/1¼ oz butter

25 g/1 oz soft light brown sugar

Method

1 Preheat the oven to 200°C/400°F/Gas Mark 6. Grease a 12-cup muffin tin or line with 12 paper cases.

2 To make the topping, sift together the flour and cinnamon into a large bowl. Cut the butter into small pieces, add to the bowl and rub it in with your fingertips until the mixture resembles fine breadcrumbs. Stir in the sugar and set aside.

3 Sift together the flour, baking powder, cinnamon and salt into a separate large bowl. Stir in the sugar. Add the apple to the flour mixture and stir together.

4 Lightly beat the eggs in a large jug, then beat in the milk and melted butter. Make a well in the centre of the dry ingredients and pour in the beaten liquid ingredients. Stir gently until just combined; do not over-mix.

5 Divide the mixture evenly between the holes in the prepared muffin tin. Scatter the streusel topping over the tops of the muffins. Bake in the preheated oven for about 20 minutes, or until well risen, golden and firm to the touch.

6 Transfer to a wire rack and leave to cool.

EVERYDAY MUFFINS

BLUEBERRY MUFFINS

Makes: 12

Prep: 20 mins, plus cooling

Cook: 20 mins

Ingredients

280 g/10 oz plain flour

1 tbsp baking powder

pinch of salt

115 g/4 oz soft light brown sugar

150 g/5½ oz blueberries

2 eggs

250 ml/9 fl oz milk

6 tbsp sunflower oil or 85 g/3 oz butter, melted, plus extra for greasing

1 tsp vanilla extract

finely grated rind of 1 lemon

Method

1 Preheat the oven to 200°C/400°F/Gas Mark 6. Grease a 12-cup muffin tin or line with 12 paper cases.

2 Sift together the flour, baking powder and salt into a large bowl. Stir in the sugar and blueberries.

3 Lightly beat the eggs in a large jug or bowl, then beat in the milk, oil, vanilla extract and lemon rind. Make a well in the centre of the dry ingredients and pour in the beaten liquid ingredients. Stir gently until just combined; do not over-mix.

4 Divide the mixture evenly between the holes in the prepared muffin tin. Bake in the preheated oven for about 20 minutes, or until well risen, golden and firm to the touch.

5 Transfer to a wire rack and leave to cool.

ROCKY ROAD MUFFINS

Makes: 12

Prep: 20 mins, plus cooling

Cook: 25 mins

Ingredients

225 g/8 oz plain flour

55 g/2 oz cocoa powder

1 tbsp baking powder

pinch of salt

115 g/4 oz caster sugar

100 g/3½ oz white chocolate chips

50 g/1¾ oz white mini marshmallows, cut in half

2 eggs

250 ml/9 fl oz milk

85 g/3 oz butter, melted and cooled , plus extra for greasing

Method

1 Preheat the oven to 200°C/400°F/Gas Mark 6. Grease a 12-cup muffin tin or line with 12 paper cases. Sift together the flour, cocoa powder, baking powder and salt into a large bowl. Stir in the sugar, chocolate chips and marshmallows.

2 Lightly beat the eggs in a large bowl then beat in the milk and butter. Make a well in the centre of the dry ingredients and pour in the beaten liquid ingredients. Gently stir until just combined; do not over-mix.

3 Divide the mixture evenly between the holes in the prepared muffin tin. Bake in the preheated oven for about 20 minutes, or until well risen and firm to the touch.

4 Transfer to a wire rack and leave to cool.

RASPBERRY CRUMBLE MUFFINS

Makes: 12

Prep: 25 mins, plus cooling

Cook: 25 mins

Ingredients

280 g/10 oz plain flour

1 tbsp baking powder

½ tsp bicarbonate of soda

pinch of salt

115 g/4 oz caster sugar

2 eggs

250 ml/9 fl oz plain yogurt

85 g/3 oz butter, melted, plus extra for greasing

1 tsp vanilla extract

150 g/5½ oz raspberries

Topping

50 g/1¾ oz plain flour

35 g/1¼ oz butter

25 g/1 oz caster sugar

Method

1 Preheat the oven to 200°C/400°F/Gas Mark 6. Grease a 12-cup muffin tin or line with 12 paper cases.

2 To make the topping, sift the flour into a bowl. Cut the butter into small pieces, add to the bowl with the flour and rub it in with your fingertips until the mixture resembles fine breadcrumbs. Stir in the sugar and set aside.

3 To make the muffins, sift together the flour, baking powder, bicarbonate of soda and salt into a large bowl. Stir in the sugar.

4 Lightly beat the eggs in a large bowl then beat in the yogurt, butter and vanilla extract. Make a well in the centre of the dry ingredients, pour in the beaten liquid ingredients and add the raspberries. Stir gently until just combined; do not over-mix.

5 Divide the mixture evenly between the holes in the prepared muffin tin. Scatter the crumble topping over each muffin and press down lightly. Bake in the preheated oven for about 20 minutes, or until well risen, golden and firm.

6 Serve warm or transfer to a wire rack and leave to cool.

PEACH MELBA MUFFINS

Makes: 12

Prep: 25 mins, plus cooling

Cook: 25–30 mins

Ingredients

280 g/10 oz self-raising flour

2 tsp baking powder

115 g/4 oz soft light brown sugar

1 large egg

150 ml/5 fl oz milk

115 g/4 oz butter, melted, plus extra for greasing

140 g/5 oz raspberries

140 g/5 oz drained canned peach slices, chopped

1 tbsp chopped mixed nuts

1 tbsp demerara sugar

Method

1 Preheat the oven to 200°C/400°F/Gas Mark 6. Grease a 12-cup muffin tin or line with 12 paper cases. Sift together the flour and baking powder into a large bowl. Stir in the brown sugar.

2 Lightly beat the egg in a large jug, then beat in the milk and melted butter. Make a well in the centre of the dry ingredients and pour in the beaten liquid ingredients. Stir gently until just combined; do not over-mix. Gently fold in the raspberries and peaches.

3 Divide the mixture evenly between the holes in the prepared muffin tin. Mix together the nuts and demerara sugar and sprinkle over the top of the muffins. Bake in the preheated oven for 20–25 minutes, or until well risen, golden and firm.

4 Serve warm or transfer to a wire rack and leave to cool.

SPICED CHOCOLATE MUFFINS

Makes: 12

Prep: 20 mins, plus cooling

Cook: 25–30 mins

Ingredients

100 g/3½ oz butter, plus extra for greasing

150 g/5½ oz caster sugar

115 g/4 oz soft light brown sugar

2 large eggs

150 ml/5 fl oz soured cream

5 tbsp milk

250 g/9 oz plain flour

1 tsp bicarbonate of soda

2 tbsp cocoa powder

1 tsp ground allspice

200 g/7 oz plain chocolate chips

Method

1 Preheat the oven to 190°C/375°F/Gas Mark 5. Grease a 12-cup muffin tin or line with 12 paper cases. Place the butter and sugars in a large bowl and beat together, then beat in the eggs, soured cream and milk until thoroughly mixed.

2 Sift together the flour, bicarbonate of soda, cocoa powder and allspice into a separate large bowl. Make a well in the centre of the dry ingredients, pour in the beaten liquid ingredients and add the chocolate chips. Stir gently until just combined; do not over-mix.

3 Divide the mixture evenly between the holes in the prepared muffin tin. Bake in the preheated oven for 25–30 minutes, or until well risen and firm.

4 Serve warm or transfer to a wire rack and leave to cool.

EVERYDAY MUFFINS

CHOCOLATE CHIP MUFFINS

Makes: 12

Prep: 20 mins, plus cooling

Cook: 20 mins

Ingredients

280 g/10 oz plain flour

1 tbsp baking powder

pinch of salt

115 g/4 oz caster sugar

175 g/6 oz milk chocolate chips

2 eggs

250 ml/9 fl oz milk

6 tbsp sunflower oil or 85 g/3 oz butter, melted, plus extra for greasing

1 tsp vanilla extract

Method

1 Preheat the oven to 200°C/400°F/Gas Mark 6. Grease a 12-cup muffin tin or line with 12 paper cases.

2 Sift together the flour, baking powder and salt into a large bowl. Stir in the sugar and chocolate chips. Lightly beat the eggs in a large jug or bowl then beat in the milk, oil and vanilla extract.

3 Make a well in the centre of the dry ingredients and pour in the beaten liquid ingredients. Stir gently until just combined; do not over-mix.

4 Divide the mixture evenly between the holes in the prepared muffin tin. Bake in the preheated oven for about 20 minutes, or until well risen, golden and firm to the touch. Serve warm or transfer to a wire rack and leave to cool.

EVERYDAY MUFFINS

MARBLED CHOCOLATE MUFFINS

Makes: 12

Prep: 20 mins, plus cooling

Cook: 25 mins

Ingredients

280 g/10 oz plain flour

1 tbsp baking powder

pinch of salt

115 g/4 oz caster sugar

2 eggs

250 ml/9 fl oz milk

85 g/3 oz butter, melted, plus extra for greasing

1 tsp vanilla extract

2 tbsp cocoa powder

Method

1 Preheat the oven to 200°C/400°F/Gas Mark 6. Grease a 12-cup muffin tin or line with 12 paper cases. Sift together the flour, baking powder and salt into a large bowl. Stir in the sugar.

2 Lightly beat the eggs in a large jug, then beat in the milk, melted butter and vanilla extract. Make a well in the centre of the dry ingredients and pour in the beaten liquid ingredients. Stir gently until just combined; do not over-mix.

3 Divide the mixture between two bowls. Sift the cocoa powder into one bowl and stir into the mixture. Using teaspoons, divide the mixtures evenly between the holes in the prepared muffin tin, alternating the chocolate mixture and the plain mixture.

4 Bake in the preheated oven for about 20 minutes, or until well risen, golden and firm to the touch.

5 Serve warm or transfer to a wire rack and leave to cool.

EVERYDAY MUFFINS

HONEY & BANANA MUFFINS

Makes: 12

Prep: 25 mins, plus cooling

Cook: 25–30 mins

Ingredients

280 g/10 oz self-raising flour

1 tsp baking powder

½ tsp bicarbonate of soda

1 tsp ground cinnamon

pinch of salt

85 g/3 oz golden granulated sugar

85 g/3 oz butter, melted, plus extra for greasing

125 ml/4 fl oz milk

2 tbsp runny honey, plus extra for brushing

1 tsp vanilla extract

2 eggs

2 ripe bananas, mashed

dried banana chips, to decorate

Method

1 Preheat the oven to 180°C/350°F/Gas Mark 4. Grease a 12-cup muffin tin or line with 12 paper cases. Sift the flour, baking powder, bicarbonate of soda, cinnamon and salt into a large bowl. Add the sugar and stir to combine.

2 In a another bowl, beat the melted butter, milk, honey, vanilla extract, eggs and mashed banana together. Make a well in the centre of the dry ingredients and pour in the beaten liquid ingredients. Stir gently until just combined; do not over-mix.

3 Divide the mixture evenly between the holes in the prepared muffin tin. Bake in the preheated oven for 20–25 minutes, or until well risen, golden and firm to the touch. Brush the top of each muffin with honey and top with a banana chip.

4 Transfer to a wire rack and leave to cool.

EVERYDAY MUFFINS

CHOCOLATE CHUNK MUFFINS

Makes: 12

Prep: 20 mins, plus cooling

Cook: 20–25 mins

Ingredients

300 g/10½ oz self-raising flour

1½ tsp baking powder

85 g/3 oz butter, plus extra for greasing

85 g/3 oz caster sugar

150 g/5½ oz plain chocolate chunks

2 large eggs

200 ml/7 fl oz buttermilk

1 tsp vanilla extract

Method

1 Preheat the oven to 200°C/400°F/Gas Mark 6. Grease a 12-cup muffin tin or line with 12 paper cases.

2 Sift together the flour and baking powder into a large bowl. Add the butter and rub in to make fine breadcrumbs. Stir in the sugar and the chocolate chunks.

3 Beat the eggs, buttermilk and vanilla extract in a large jug or bowl. Make a well in the centre of the dry ingredients and pour in the beaten liquid ingredients. Stir gently until just combined; do not over-mix.

4 Divide the mixture evenly between the holes in the prepared muffin tin. Bake in the preheated oven for 20–25 minutes, or until well risen, golden and firm to the touch. Transfer to a wire rack and leave to cool.

RAISIN BRAN MUFFINS

Makes: 12

Prep: 20 mins, plus cooling

Cook: 20 mins

Ingredients

140 g/5 oz plain flour

1 tbsp baking powder

140 g/5 oz wheat bran

115 g/4 oz caster sugar

150 g/5½ oz raisins

2 eggs

250 ml/9 fl oz skimmed milk

6 tbsp sunflower oil, plus extra for greasing

1 tsp vanilla extract

Method

1 Preheat the oven to 200°C/400°F/Gas Mark 6. Grease a 12-cup muffin tin or line with 12 paper cases. Sift the flour and baking powder together into a large bowl. Stir in the bran, sugar and raisins.

2 Lightly beat the eggs in a large jug or bowl, then beat in the milk, oil and vanilla extract. Make a well in the centre of the dry ingredients and pour in the beaten liquid ingredients. Stir gently until just combined; do not over-mix.

3 Divide the mixture evenly between the holes in the prepared muffin tin. Bake in the preheated oven for about 20 minutes, or until well risen, golden and firm to the touch.

4 Serve warm or transfer to a wire rack and leave to cool.

GLUTEN-FREE BLUEBERRY & OATMEAL MUFFINS

Makes: 9   **Prep: 20 mins,** plus cooling   **Cook: 20–25 mins**

Ingredients

250 ml/9 fl oz orange juice

60 g/2¼ oz gluten-free porridge oats

100 g/3½ oz caster sugar

200 g/7 oz gluten-free plain flour, sifted

½ tsp xanthan gum

1½ tsp gluten-free baking powder

½ tsp gluten-free bicarbonate of soda

½ tsp ground cinnamon

¼ tsp ground mixed spice

125 ml/4 fl oz vegetable oil, plus extra for greasing

1 egg, beaten

1 tsp glycerine

175 g/6 oz blueberries

demerara sugar, to sprinkle

Method

1 Preheat the oven to 180°C/350°F/Gas Mark 4. Grease a 9-cup muffin tin or line with 9 paper cases.

2 Add the orange juice to the porridge oats and mix well in a bowl.

3 In a separate bowl, mix the sugar, flour, xanthan gum, baking powder, bicarbonate of soda and spices. Add the oil, egg and glycerine to the dry mixture and mix well. Then add the oat mixture and blueberries and fold these in gently.

4 Divide the mixture evenly between the holes in the prepared muffin tin and sprinkle with demerara sugar.

5 Bake in the preheated oven for 20–25 minutes, or until well risen, golden and firm to the touch. Transfer to a wire rack and leave to cool.

CHOCOLATE & SOUR CHERRY MUFFINS

Makes: 12

Prep: 25 mins, plus cooling

Cook: 25–30 mins

Ingredients

225 g/8 oz plain flour

1 tbsp baking powder

40 g/1½ oz cocoa powder

115 g/4 oz soft light brown sugar

85 g/3 oz butter, chilled and coarsely grated, plus extra for greasing

2 eggs

175 ml/6 fl oz milk

55 g/2 oz dried sour cherries

1 tbsp plain chocolate shavings

Frosting

55 g/2 oz plain chocolate, broken into pieces

25 g/1 oz butter

Method

1 Preheat the oven to 200°C/400°F/Gas Mark 6. Grease a 12-cup muffin tin or line with 12 paper cases. Sift together the flour, baking powder and cocoa powder into a large bowl. Stir in the sugar. Add the grated butter and stir with a fork to coat in the flour mixture.

2 Lightly beat the eggs in a large jug, then beat in the milk. Make a well in the centre of the dry ingredients and pour in the beaten liquid ingredients. Stir gently until just combined; do not over-mix. Gently fold in the dried cherries.

3 Divide the mixture evenly between the holes in the prepared muffin tin. Bake in the preheated oven for 20–25 minutes, or until well risen and firm to the touch.

4 Transfer to a wire rack and leave to cool.

5 To make the frosting, melt the chocolate with the butter in a heatproof bowl set over a saucepan of gently simmering water. Leave to cool for 15 minutes, then spoon over the tops of the muffins and sprinkle with the chocolate shavings.

PUMPKIN & PECAN MUFFINS

Makes: 18

Prep: 20 mins, plus cooling

Cook: 25–30 mins

Ingredients

175 g/6 oz muscovado sugar

2 eggs

55 g/2 oz butter, melted, plus extra for greasing

250 g/9 oz canned pumpkin or cooked pumpkin, mashed

125 ml/4 fl oz buttermilk

250 g/9 oz plain flour

2 tsp baking powder

1 tsp ground cinnamon

1 tsp ground mixed spice

½ tsp salt

¼ tsp ground cloves

55 g/2 oz pecan nuts, chopped

85 g/3 oz raisins

Method

1 Preheat the oven to 200°C/400°F/Gas Mark 6. Grease three 6-cup muffin tins or line with 18 paper cases. Beat the sugar, eggs and butter in a large bowl and mix until the sugar dissolves. Add the pumpkin and buttermilk and stir until smooth.

2 Mix the flour, baking powder, cinnamon, mixed spice, salt, cloves, pecan nuts and raisins in a large bowl. Make a well in the centre of the dry ingredients and pour in the beaten liquid ingredients. Stir gently until just combined; do not over-mix.

3 Divide the mixture evenly between the holes in the prepared muffin tin. Bake in the preheated oven for 20–25 minutes, or until well risen, golden and firm to the touch.

4 Transfer to a wire rack and leave to cool.

WHITE CHOCOLATE & HAZELNUT MUFFINS

Makes: 10

Prep: 25 mins, plus cooling

Cook: 25–30 mins

Ingredients

200 g/7 oz plain flour

1 tbsp baking powder

55 g/2 oz ground hazelnuts

115 g/4 oz caster sugar

85 g/3 oz butter, chilled and coarsely grated, plus extra for greasing

1 large egg

175 ml/6 fl oz milk

140 g/5 oz white chocolate

15 g/½ oz hazelnuts, roughly chopped

Method

1 Preheat the oven to 200°C/400°F/Gas Mark 6. Grease a 10-cup muffin tin or line with 10 paper cases. Sift together the flour and baking powder into a large bowl. Stir in the ground hazelnuts and sugar. Add the grated butter and stir with a fork to coat in the flour mixture.

2 Lightly beat the egg in a large jug, then beat in the milk. Make a well in the centre of the dry ingredients and pour in the beaten liquid ingredients. Stir gently until just combined; do not over-mix. Roughly chop 85 g/3 oz of the chocolate and fold into the mixture.

3 Divide the mixture evenly between the holes in the prepared muffin tin. Bake in the preheated oven for 20–25 minutes, or until well risen, golden and firm to the touch.

4 Transfer to a wire rack and leave to cool.

5 Melt the remaining chocolate in a heatproof bowl set over a saucepan of gently simmering water. Drizzle the melted chocolate over the muffins and sprinkle with the chopped hazelnuts.

APPLE & RASPBERRY MUFFINS

Makes: 12

Prep: 30 mins, plus cooling

Cook: 45–50 mins

Ingredients

3 large cooking apples, peeled

450 ml/16 fl oz water

1½ tsp ground allspice

oil or melted butter, for greasing (if using)

300 g/10½ oz plain wholemeal flour

1 tbsp baking powder

¼ tsp salt

3 tbsp caster sugar

85 g/3 oz raspberries

Method

1 Thinly slice two of the apples and place them in a saucepan with 6 tablespoons of the water. Bring to the boil, then reduce the heat. Stir in ½ teaspoon of the allspice, cover and simmer, stirring occasionally, for 15–20 minutes. Remove from the heat and leave to cool. Blend in a food processor until smooth. Stir in the remaining water.

2 Preheat the oven to 200°C/400°F/Gas Mark 6. Grease a 12-cup muffin tin or line with 12 paper cases. Sift together the flour, baking powder, salt and the remaining allspice into a large bowl, adding any husks that remain in the sieve. Stir in the sugar.

3 Chop the remaining apple and add to the bowl with the raspberries and apple purée. Gently stir until just combined; do not over-mix.

4 Divide the mixture evenly between the holes in the prepared muffin tin. Bake in the preheated oven for 25 minutes, or until well risen, golden and firm to the touch.

5 Serve warm or transfer to a wire rack and leave to cool.

MINT CHOCOLATE CHIP MUFFINS

Makes: 12

Prep: 20 mins, plus cooling

Cook: 25 mins

Ingredients

280 g/10 oz plain flour

1 tbsp baking powder

pinch of salt

115 g/4 oz caster sugar

150 g/5½ oz plain chocolate chips

2 eggs

250 ml/9 fl oz milk

85 g/3 oz butter, melted, plus extra for greasing

1 tsp peppermint extract

a few drops of green food colouring (optional)

icing sugar, for dusting

Method

1 Preheat the oven to 200°C/400°F/Gas Mark 6. Grease a 12-cup muffin tin or line with 12 paper cases. Sift together the flour, baking powder and salt into a large bowl. Stir in the caster sugar and chocolate chips.

2 Lightly beat the eggs in a large jug, then beat in the milk, melted butter and peppermint extract. Add the food colouring, if using, to colour the mixture a very subtle shade of green. Make a well in the centre of the dry ingredients and pour in the beaten liquid ingredients. Stir gently until just combined; do not over-mix.

3 Divide the mixture evenly between the holes in the prepared muffin tin. Bake in the preheated oven for about 20 minutes, or until well risen, golden and firm to the touch.

4 Serve warm or transfer to a wire rack and leave to cool. Dust with icing sugar before serving.

RHUBARB & GINGER MUFFINS

Makes: 12

Prep: 25 mins, plus cooling

Cook: 20–25 mins

Ingredients

200 g/7 oz plain flour

2 tsp baking powder

115 g/4 oz caster sugar

2 eggs

100 ml/3½ fl oz milk

125 g/4½ oz butter, melted, plus extra for greasing

250 g/9 oz rhubarb, cut into 1-cm/½-inch lengths

3 tbsp raisins

2 pieces of stem ginger in syrup, drained and chopped

Method

1 Preheat the oven to 180°C/350°F/Gas Mark 4. Grease a 12-cup muffin tin or line with 12 paper cases.

2 Sift together the flour and baking powder into a large bowl. Stir in the sugar. Lightly beat the eggs in a large jug, then beat in the milk and melted butter. Make a well in the centre of the dry ingredients and pour in the beaten liquid ingredients. Stir in the rhubarb, raisins and stem ginger until just combined; do not over-mix.

3 Divide the mixture evenly between the holes in the prepared muffin tin. Bake in the preheated oven for 15–20 minutes, or until well risen, golden and firm to the touch.

4 Serve warm or transfer to a wire rack and leave to cool.

EVERYDAY MUFFINS

TRIPLE CHOCOLATE MUFFINS

Makes: 12

Prep: 20 mins,
plus cooling

Cook: 25 mins

Ingredients

250 g/9 oz plain flour

25 g/1 oz cocoa powder

2 tsp baking powder

½ tsp bicarbonate of soda

100 g/3½ oz plain chocolate chips

100 g/3½ oz white chocolate chips

85 g/3 oz light muscovado sugar

2 eggs

300 ml/10 fl oz soured cream

85 g/3 oz butter, melted, plus extra for greasing

Method

1 Preheat the oven to 200°C/400°F/Gas Mark 6. Grease a 12-cup muffin tin or line with 12 paper cases. Sift together the flour, cocoa powder, baking powder and bicarbonate of soda into a large bowl, then stir in the chocolate chips and sugar.

2 Lightly beat the eggs in a large jug, then beat in the soured cream and melted butter. Make a well in the centre of the dry ingredients and pour in the beaten liquid ingredients. Stir gently until just combined; do not over-mix.

3 Divide the mixture evenly between the holes in the prepared muffin tin. Bake in the preheated oven for 20 minutes, or until well risen and firm to the touch.

4 Serve warm or transfer to a wire rack and leave to cool.

APRICOT & MACADAMIA MUFFINS

Makes: 12

Prep: 25 mins, plus cooling

Cook: 20–25 mins

Ingredients

280 g/10 oz plain flour

1 tbsp baking powder

115 g/4 oz golden caster sugar

85 g/3 oz ready-to-eat dried apricots, chopped

55 g/2 oz macadamia nuts, chopped

55 g/2 oz white chocolate, chopped

2 eggs

200 ml/7 fl oz buttermilk

100 ml/3½ fl oz sunflower oil, plus extra for greasing

Method

1 Preheat the oven to 200°C/400°F/Gas Mark 6. Grease a 12-cup muffin tin or line with 12 paper cases.

2 Sift the flour and baking powder into a bowl and stir in the sugar, apricots, nuts and chocolate.

3 Beat together the eggs, buttermilk and oil in a large jug or bowl. Make a well in the centre of the dry ingredients and pour in the beaten liquid ingredients. Stir gently until just combined; do not over-mix.

4 Divide the mixture evenly between the holes in the prepared muffin tin. Bake in the preheated oven for 20–25 minutes, or until well risen, golden and firm to the touch.

5 Serve warm or transfer to a wire rack and leave to cool.

GLUTEN-FREE APPLE & CINNAMON MUFFINS

Makes: 12

Prep: 20 mins, plus cooling

Cook: 20–25 mins

Ingredients

4 tbsp vegetable oil, plus extra for greasing

1 tbsp glycerine

175 g/6 oz apple purée

2 eggs

½ tsp vanilla extract

55 g/2 oz runny honey

75 ml/2½ fl oz milk

300 g/10½ oz gluten-free plain flour

120 g/4¼ oz gluten-free oat bran

70 g/2½ oz ground linseeds

1 tsp gluten-free baking powder

½ tsp gluten-free bicarbonate of soda

½ tsp xanthan gum

1 tsp cinnamon

¼ tsp mixed spice

175 g/6 oz soft brown sugar

125 g/4½ oz raisins and sultanas

Method

1 Preheat the oven to 180°C/350°F/Gas Mark 4. Grease a 12-cup muffin tin or line with 12 paper cases.

2 In a large bowl, whisk together the vegetable oil, glycerine, apple purée, eggs, vanilla extract, honey and milk. In a separate bowl, mix all the dry ingredients together then add the liquid mixture and stir well.

3 Divide the mixture evenly between the holes of the prepared muffin tin. Bake the muffins in the preheated oven for 20–25 minutes, or until well risen, golden and firm to the touch.

4 Serve warm or transfer to a wire rack and leave to cool.

CHOCOLATE & CINNAMON MUFFINS

Makes: 12

Prep: 20 mins, plus cooling

Cook: 25 mins

Ingredients

225 g/8 oz plain flour

55 g/2 oz cocoa powder

1 tbsp baking powder

½ tsp ground cinnamon

pinch of salt

115 g/4 oz soft light brown sugar

150 g/5½ oz plain chocolate chips

2 eggs

250 ml/9 fl oz milk

85 g/3 oz butter, melted, plus extra for greasing

Method

1 Preheat the oven to 200°C/400°F/Gas Mark 6. Grease a 12-cup muffin tin or line with 12 paper cases. Sift together the flour, cocoa powder, baking powder, cinnamon and salt into a large bowl. Stir in the sugar and chocolate chips.

2 Lightly beat the eggs in a large jug, then beat in the milk and melted butter. Make a well in the centre of the dry ingredients and pour in the beaten liquid ingredients. Stir gently until just combined; do not over-mix.

3 Divide the mixture evenly between the holes of the prepared muffin tin. Bake in the preheated oven for about 20 minutes, or until well risen and firm to the touch.

4 Serve warm or transfer to a wire rack and leave to cool.

★ **Variation**

If you like a spicier flavour, replace the cinnamon with a pinch of chilli powder, or to taste.

SOMETHING SPECIAL MUFFINS

JAM DOUGHNUT MUFFINS

Makes: 12

Prep: 25 mins, plus cooling

Cook: 20 mins

Ingredients

280 g/10 oz plain flour

1 tbsp baking powder

pinch of salt

115 g/4 oz caster sugar

2 eggs

200 ml/7 fl oz milk

6 tbsp sunflower oil or 85 g/3 oz butter, plus extra for greasing

1 tsp vanilla extract

4 tbsp strawberry jam or raspberry jam

Topping

115 g/4 oz butter

150 g/5½ oz granulated sugar

Method

1 Preheat the oven to 200°C/400°F/Gas Mark 6. Grease a 12-cup muffin tin or line with 12 paper cases.

2 Sift together the flour, baking powder and salt into a large bowl. Stir in the caster sugar. Lightly beat the eggs in a large jug then beat in the milk, oil and vanilla extract. Make a well in the centre of the dry ingredients and pour in the beaten liquid ingredients. Stir gently until just combined; do not over-mix.

3 Spoon half of the mixture into the holes in the prepared muffin tin. Add a teaspoon of jam to the centre of each, then cover with the remaining mixture. Bake in the preheated oven for about 20 minutes, or until well risen, golden and firm to the touch.

4 Meanwhile, prepare the topping. Melt the butter. Spread the granulated sugar in a wide, shallow bowl. When the muffins are baked, leave in the tin for 5 minutes. Dip the tops of the muffins in the melted butter then roll in the sugar. Serve warm or transfer to a wire rack and leave to cool.

★ **Variation**

These doughnuts can be filled with apple sauce instead of jam to make apple doughnuts.

IRISH COFFEE MUFFINS

Makes: 12

Prep: 25 mins,
plus cooling & chilling

Cook: 20 mins

Ingredients

280 g/10 oz plain flour

1 tbsp baking powder

pinch of salt

85 g/3 oz butter, plus extra for greasing

55 g/2 oz soft light brown sugar

1 large egg, beaten

125 ml/4 fl oz double cream

1 tsp almond extract

2 tbsp strong coffee

2 tbsp coffee-flavoured liqueur

4 tbsp Irish whiskey

whipped cream and cocoa powder, to serve (optional)

Method

1 Preheat the oven to 200°C/400°F/Gas Mark 6. Grease a 12-cup muffin tin or line with 12 paper cases. Sift together the flour, baking powder and salt into a large bowl.

2 In a separate large bowl, cream together the butter and sugar, then stir in the egg. Mix in the double cream, almond extract, coffee, liqueur and whiskey. Make a well in the centre of the dry ingredients and pour in the liquid ingredients. Stir gently until just combined; do not over-mix.

3 Divide the mixture evenly between the holes in the prepared muffin tin. Bake in the preheated oven for 20 minutes, or until well risen, golden and firm to the touch.

4 Transfer to a wire rack and leave to cool. If liked, pipe a swirl of whipped cream over the top of each muffin and dust with cocoa powder. Chill the muffins in the refrigerator until ready to serve.

CHERRY & BRANDY MUFFINS

Makes: 12

Prep: 20 mins, plus cooling

Cook: 20–25 mins

Ingredients

225 g/8 oz plain flour

1 tbsp baking powder

pinch of salt

40 g/1½ oz butter, plus extra for greasing

2 tbsp caster sugar

1 egg, beaten

200 ml/7 fl oz milk

2 tsp cherry brandy

300 g/10½ oz drained canned cherries, chopped

Method

1 Preheat the oven to 200°C/400°F/Gas Mark 6. Grease a 12-cup muffin tin or line with 12 paper cases. Sift together the flour, baking powder and salt into a large bowl.

2 In a separate large bowl, cream together the butter and sugar, then stir in the egg. Pour in the milk and cherry brandy, then add the cherries and gently stir together. Make a well in the centre of the dry ingredients and pour in the liquid ingredients. Stir gently until just combined; do not over-mix.

3 Divide the mixture evenly between the holes in the prepared muffin tin. Bake in the preheated oven for 20–25 minutes, or until well risen, golden and firm to the touch.

4 Serve warm or transfer to a wire rack and leave to cool.

VEGAN MANGO & COCONUT MUFFINS

Makes: 10

Prep: 25 mins, plus cooling

Cook: 25–30 mins

Ingredients

250 g/9 oz plain flour

1 tbsp baking powder

1 tbsp linseed meal

55 g/2 oz desiccated coconut, plus 2 tbsp for topping

125 g/4½ oz caster sugar

9 cardamom pods

175 ml/6 fl oz soya milk

5 tbsp rapeseed oil, plus extra for greasing

250 g/9 oz fresh, ripe mango, chopped

Method

1 Preheat the oven to 190°C/375°F/Gas Mark 5. Grease a 10-cup muffin tin or line with 10 paper cases.

2 Sift together the flour and baking powder into a large bowl. Mix in the linseed meal, coconut and sugar.

3 Crush the cardamom pods and remove the seeds. Discard the green pods. Crush the seeds finely in a pestle and mortar or with a rolling pin and stir into the mixture.

4 Whisk together the soya milk and oil in a small bowl and stir into the mixture, adding the mango at the same time. Mix until just combined; do not over-mix.

5 Divide the mixture evenly between the holes in the prepared muffin tin. Sprinkle the top of each muffin with a little of the extra coconut. Bake in the preheated oven for 25–30 minutes, or until well risen, golden and firm to the touch. Transfer to a wire rack and leave to cool.

CRANBERRY & PARMESAN MUFFINS

Makes: 18

Prep: 20 mins, plus cooling

Cook: 25 mins

Ingredients

225 g/8 oz plain flour

2 tsp baking powder

½ tsp salt

55 g/2 oz caster sugar

2 large eggs

175 ml/6 fl oz milk

55 g/2 oz butter, melted, plus extra for greasing

115 g/4 oz fresh cranberries

25 g/1 oz freshly grated Parmesan cheese

Method

1 Preheat the oven to 200°C/400°F/Gas Mark 6. Grease two muffin tins or line the tins with 18 paper cases. Sift together the flour, baking powder and salt into a large bowl. Stir in the sugar.

2 Lightly beat the eggs in a large jug, then beat in the milk and melted butter. Make a well in the centre of the dry ingredients, pour in the beaten liquid ingredients and add the cranberries. Stir gently until just combined; do not over-mix.

3 Divide the mixture evenly between the holes in the prepared muffin tin. Sprinkle the Parmesan cheese over the tops of the muffins. Bake in the preheated oven for 20 minutes, or until well risen, golden and firm to the touch.

4 Serve warm or transfer to a wire rack and leave to cool.

PECAN BROWNIE MUFFINS

Makes: 12

Prep: 25 mins, plus cooling

Cook: 25–30 mins

Ingredients

115 g/4 oz pecan nuts

100 g/3½ oz plain flour

175 g/6 oz caster sugar

¼ tsp salt

1 tbsp baking powder

225 g/8 oz butter, plus extra for greasing

115 g/4 oz plain chocolate, broken into pieces

4 eggs, lightly beaten

1 tsp vanilla extract

Method

1. Preheat the oven to 200°C/400°F/Gas Mark 6. Grease a 12-cup muffin tin or line with 12 paper cases. Reserve 12 pecan halves and roughly chop the rest.

2. Sift together the flour, sugar, salt and baking powder into a large bowl and make a well in the centre. Melt the butter and chocolate in a heatproof bowl set over a pan of gently simmering water. Add to the dry ingredients and stir to mix evenly.

3. Add the eggs and vanilla extract. Stir gently until just combined; do not over-mix. Stir in the chopped pecan nuts.

4. Divide the mixture evenly between the holes in the prepared muffin tin. Top each muffin with one of the reserved pecan nut halves. Bake in the preheated oven for 20–25 minutes, or until well risen and firm to the touch.

5. Serve warm or transfer to a wire rack and leave to cool.

SOMETHING SPECIAL MUFFINS

MINI MUFFINS WITH TOFFEE SAUCE

Makes: 20

Prep: 25 mins, plus cooling

Cook: 42–45 mins

Ingredients

)0 g/7 oz ready-to-eat dried dates, stoned and chopped

200 ml/7 fl oz water

1 tsp bicarbonate of soda

55 g/2 oz butter, plus extra for greasing

175 g/6 oz self-raising flour

150 g/5½ oz caster sugar

1 tsp vanilla extract

2 eggs, lightly beaten

Toffee sauce

150 ml/5 fl oz double cream

1 tbsp golden syrup

70 g/2½ oz soft light brown sugar

55 g/2 oz butter

Method

1 Preheat the oven to 180°C/350°F/Gas Mark 4. Grease two mini muffin tins or line with 20 paper cases.

2 Put the dates and water in a saucepan and bring to the boil. Cook over a low heat for 10 minutes, or until softened. Stir in the bicarbonate of soda and butter – it will froth up – and stir until the butter has melted. Leave to cool slightly, then pour the mixture into a blender or food processor and process to a coarse purée.

3 Sift the flour into a large bowl and stir in the caster sugar. Make a well in the centre of the dry ingredients and add the vanilla extract, eggs and date purée. Stir gently until just combined; do not over-mix.

4 Divide the mixture evenly between the holes in the prepared muffin tin. Bake in the preheated oven for 12–15 minutes, or until well risen and firm to the touch.

5 To make the sauce, put all the ingredients in a small saucepan. Bring to the boil, stirring constantly, then simmer for 10 minutes, or until thickened and glossy. Remove from the heat and leave to cool slightly. Serve the muffins warm with the sauce.

SOMETHING SPECIAL MUFFINS

GLUTEN-FREE CHOCOLATE FUDGE MUFFINS

Makes: 12   **Prep: 30 mins,** plus cooling   **Cook: 25–30 mins**

Ingredients

50 g/1¾ oz gluten-free plain chocolate, broken into pieces

175 g/6 oz butter, plus extra for greasing

175 g/6 oz caster sugar

3 eggs

½ tsp vanilla extract

½ tsp glycerine

175 g/6 oz gluten-free self-raising flour

½ tsp gluten-free baking powder

1 tsp xanthan gum

40 g/1½ oz ground almonds

Frosting

90 g/3¼ oz gluten-free plain chocolate, broken into pieces

120 g/4¼ oz butter

450 g/1 lb gluten-free icing sugar

185 ml/6½ fl oz milk

½ tsp vanilla extract

Method

1 Preheat the oven to 180°C/350°F/Gas Mark 4. Grease a 12-cup muffin tin or line with 12 paper cases.

2 Melt the chocolate in a heatproof bowl set over a pan of simmering water. In a separate bowl, beat the butter and caster sugar together, then beat in the eggs, one at a time, and add the vanilla extract and glycerine. Once the chocolate has cooled slightly, add it to the butter and egg mixture.

3 Sift the flour, baking powder and xanthan gum into a bowl and add the almonds. Stir the dry mixture gently into the chocolate mixture.

4 Divide the mixture evenly between the holes in the prepared muffin tin. Bake in the preheated oven for 15–20 minutes, or until well risen and firm to the touch. Transfer to a wire rack and leave to cool.

5 To make the frosting, melt the chocolate and butter in a heatproof bowl set over a pan of simmering water. Mix the icing sugar, half the milk and vanilla extract in a separate bowl and slowly add the chocolate mixture. Add the rest of the milk to get the desired consistency. Place the frosting in a piping bag and decorate each muffin when completely cool.

SOMETHING SPECIAL MUFFINS

PISTACHIO & LIME MUFFINS

Makes: 12

Prep: 20 mins, plus cooling

Cook: 20–25 mins

Ingredients

225 g/8 oz plain flour

1 tbsp baking powder

115 g/4 oz butter, chilled and diced, plus extra for greasing

150 g/5 oz caster sugar

finely grated rind and juice of 1 lime

55 g/2 oz pistachio nuts, chopped

2 eggs

100 ml/4 fl oz buttermilk

Method

1 Preheat the oven to 200°C/400°F/Gas Mark 6. Grease a 12-cup muffin tin or line with 12 paper cases.

2 Sift together the flour and baking powder into a large bowl. Add the butter and rub in with your fingertips until the mixture resembles fine breadcrumbs. Stir in the sugar, lime rind and nearly all of the pistachio nuts.

3 Lightly beat the eggs in a large jug, then beat in the buttermilk and lime juice. Make a well in the centre of the dry ingredients and pour in the beaten liquid ingredients. Stir gently until just combined; do not over-mix.

4 Divide the mixture evenly between the holes in the prepared muffin tin. Sprinkle the remaining pistachio nuts over the tops of the muffins. Bake in the preheated oven for 20–25 minutes, or until well risen, golden and firm to the touch.

5 Transfer to a wire rack and leave to cool.

MARSHMALLOW & CRANBERRY MINI MUFFINS

Makes: 48

Prep: 25 mins, plus cooling

Cook: 12–15 mins

Ingredients

200 g/7 oz plain flour

1 tbsp baking powder

85 g/3 oz light muscovado sugar

100 g/3½ oz dried cranberries

25 g/1 oz mini marshmallows

finely grated rind of ½ small lemon

1 tbsp lemon juice

1 egg

100 ml/3½ fl oz skimmed milk

3 tbsp sunflower oil, plus extra for greasing

½ tsp vanilla extract

Method

1 Preheat the oven to 200°C/400°F/Gas Mark 6. Grease four 12-cup mini muffin tins or line with 48 paper cases.

2 Sift together the flour, baking powder and sugar into a bowl. Stir in the cranberries and marshmallows.

3 Whisk together lemon rind and juice, egg, milk, oil and vanilla in a bowl. Make a well in the centre of the dry ingredients and pour in the beaten liquid ingredients. Stir gently until just combined; do not over-mix.

4 Divide the mixture evenly between the holes in the prepared muffin tin. Bake in the preheated oven for 12–15 minutes, or until well risen, golden and firm to the touch. Transfer to a wire rack and leave to cool.

CHOCOLATE DESSERT MUFFINS

Makes: 12

Prep: 25 mins, plus cooling

Cook: 25 mins

Ingredients

225 g/8 oz plain flour

55 g/2 oz cocoa powder

1 tbsp baking powder

pinch of salt

115 g/4 oz soft light brown sugar

2 eggs

250 ml/9 fl oz single cream

85 g/3 oz butter, melted, plus extra for greasing

85 g/3 oz plain chocolate

Chocolate sauce

200 g/7 oz plain chocolate, broken into pieces

25 g/1 oz butter

50 ml/2 fl oz single cream

Method

1 Preheat the oven to 200°C/400°F/Gas Mark 6. Grease a 12-cup muffin tin or line with 12 paper cases. Sift together the flour, cocoa powder, baking powder and salt into a large bowl. Stir in the sugar.

2 Lightly beat the eggs in a large jug, then beat in the cream and melted butter. Make a well in the centre of the dry ingredients and pour in the beaten liquid ingredients. Stir gently until just combined; do not over-mix.

3 Break the chocolate evenly into 12 pieces. Spoon half of the mixture into the holes in the prepared muffin tin. Place a piece of chocolate in the centre of each cup, then spoon in the remaining mixture. Bake in the preheated oven for about 20 minutes, or until well risen and firm to the touch.

4 Meanwhile, make the sauce. Melt the chocolate and butter in a heatproof bowl set over a pan of gently simmering water. Stir until blended, then add the cream and mix together. Remove from the heat and stir until smooth.

5 Serve the muffins warm with the sauce.

SOMETHING SPECIAL MUFFINS

COFFEE LIQUEUR MUFFINS

Makes: 12

Prep: 20 mins, plus cooling

Cook: 25 mins

Ingredients

2 tbsp instant coffee granules

2 tbsp boiling water

280 g/10 oz plain flour

1 tbsp baking powder

pinch of salt

115 g/4 oz soft light brown sugar

2 eggs

100 ml/3½ fl oz milk

85 g/3 oz butter, melted, plus extra for greasing

6 tbsp coffee liqueur

40 g/1½ oz demerara sugar

Method

1 Preheat the oven to 200°C/400°F/Gas Mark 6. Grease a 12-cup muffin tin or line with 12 paper cases. Put the coffee granules and boiling water in a cup and stir until dissolved. Leave to cool.

2 Sift together the flour, baking powder and salt into a large bowl. Stir in the brown sugar.

3 Lightly beat the eggs in a large jug, then beat in the milk, melted butter, coffee and liqueur. Make a well in the centre of the dry ingredients and pour in the beaten liquid ingredients. Stir gently until just combined; do not over-mix.

4 Divide the mixture evenly between the holes in the prepared muffin tin. Sprinkle the demerara sugar over the tops of the muffins. Bake in the preheated oven for about 20 minutes, or until well risen, golden and firm to the touch.

5 Serve warm or transfer to a wire rack and leave to cool.

SOMETHING SPECIAL MUFFINS

STRAWBERRY & CREAM MUFFINS

Makes: 12

Prep: 30 mins, plus cooling

Cook: 25–30 mins

Ingredients

225 g/8 oz plain flour

1 tsp baking powder

140 g/5 oz golden caster sugar

100 ml/3½ fl oz milk

2 large eggs

140 g/5 oz butter, melted, plus extra for greasing

4 tbsp strawberry jam

6 strawberries, halved, to decorate

Frosting

50 g/1¾ oz butter

85 g/3 oz icing sugar

½ tsp vanilla extract

1–2 tsp milk

Method

1 Preheat the oven to 200°C/400°F/Gas Mark 6. Grease a 12-cup muffin tin or line with 12 paper cases.

2 Sift the flour and baking powder into a large bowl. Stir in the caster sugar using a wooden spoon. Put the milk, eggs and melted butter in a jug and whisk together with a balloon whisk. Pour a little at a time into the dry ingredients, stirring gently until combined; do not over-mix.

3 Spoon a tablespoon of the muffin mixture into the holes in the prepared muffin tin, then add a teaspoon of jam. Top with the rest of the mixture.

4 Bake in the preheated oven for 20–25 minutes, or until well risen, golden and firm to the touch. Transfer to a wire rack and leave to cool.

5 For the frosting, beat together the butter, icing sugar, vanilla extract and milk in a bowl.

6 Place a spoonful of the frosting on top of each muffin, then decorate with a strawberry half.

SOMETHING SPECIAL MUFFINS

CHOCOLATE HEART MUFFINS

Makes: 12

Prep: 40 mins, plus drying & cooling

Cook: 30 mins

Ingredients

70 g/2½ oz marzipan, coloured with red food colouring

225 g/8 oz plain flour

55 g/2 oz cocoa powder

1 tbsp baking powder

pinch of salt

115 g/4 oz light brown sugar

2 eggs

250 ml/9 fl oz buttermilk

85 g/3 oz butter, melted, plus extra for greasing

icing sugar, for dusting

Frosting

55 g/2 oz plain chocolate

115 g/4 oz butter, softened

225 g/8 oz icing sugar

Method

1 To make the marzipan hearts, dust a work surface with icing sugar and roll out the marzipan to a thickness of 5 mm/¼ inch. Using a small heart-shaped cutter, cut out 12 hearts. Line a tray with baking paper, dust with icing sugar and leave the hearts there for 3–4 hours, or until dry.

2 Preheat the oven to 200°C/400°F/Gas Mark 6. Grease a 12-cup heart-shaped muffin tin. Sift the flour, cocoa powder, baking powder and salt into a large bowl. Stir in the brown sugar.

3 Lightly beat the eggs in a large jug, then beat in the buttermilk and melted butter. Make a well in the centre of the dry ingredients and pour in the beaten liquid ingredients. Stir gently until just combined; do not over-mix. Divide the mixture evenly between the holes in the prepared muffin tin. Bake in the preheated oven for about 20 minutes, or until well risen and firm to the touch. Transfer to a wire rack and leave to cool.

4 To make the frosting, melt the chocolate in a heatproof bowl set over a saucepan of gently simmering water. Put the butter in a large bowl and beat until fluffy. Sift in the icing sugar and beat until creamy. Add the chocolate and beat together. Spread the frosting onto the muffins, then decorate each with a marzipan heart.

SOMETHING SPECIAL MUFFINS

FRESH FLOWER MUFFINS

Makes: 12

Prep: 30 mins, plus cooling

Cook: 25 mins

Ingredients

280 g/10 oz plain flour

1 tbsp baking powder

pinch of salt

115 g/4 oz caster sugar

2 eggs

250 ml/9 fl oz buttermilk

85 g/3 oz butter, melted, plus extra for greasing

finely grated rind of 1 lemon

12 edible flower heads, such as lavender, violets, or roses, to decorate

Frosting

85 g/3 oz butter, softened

175 g/6 oz icing sugar

Method

1 Preheat the oven to 200°C/400°F/Gas Mark 6. Grease a 12-cup muffin tin or line with 12 paper cases.

2 Sift together the flour, baking powder and salt into a large bowl. Stir in the caster sugar.

3 Lightly beat the eggs in a large jug, then beat in the buttermilk, melted butter and lemon rind. Make a well in the centre of the dry ingredients and pour in the beaten liquid ingredients. Stir gently until just combined; do not over-mix.

4 Divide the mixture evenly between the holes in the prepared muffin tin. Bake in the preheated oven for about 20 minutes, or until well risen, golden and firm to the touch.

5 Transfer to a wire rack and leave to cool. Carefully wash the flower heads and leave to dry on kitchen paper.

6 To make the frosting, put the butter in a large bowl and beat until fluffy. Sift in the icing sugar and beat together until smooth and creamy. Spoon the frosting into a piping bag fitted with a large star nozzle and pipe a swirl on top of each muffin. Just before serving, place a flower head on top of each muffin to decorate.

SOMETHING SPECIAL MUFFINS

MARZIPAN MUFFINS

Makes: 12

Prep: 25 mins, plus cooling

Cook: 25 mins

Ingredients

175 g/6 oz marzipan
280 g/10 oz plain flour
1 tbsp baking powder
pinch of salt
115 g/4 oz caster sugar
2 eggs
200 ml/7 fl oz milk
85 g/3 oz butter, melted, plus extra for greasing
1 tsp almond extract
12 whole blanched almonds

Method

1 Preheat the oven to 200°C/400°F/Gas Mark 6. Grease a 12-cup muffin tin or line with 12 paper cases. Cut the marzipan into 12 equal pieces. Roll each piece into a ball, then flatten, making sure that it is no larger than the muffin cup.

2 Sift together the flour, baking powder and salt into a large bowl. Stir in the sugar.

3 Lightly beat the eggs in a large jug, then beat in the milk, melted butter and almond extract. Make a well in the centre of the dry ingredients and pour in the beaten liquid ingredients. Stir gently until just combined; do not over-mix.

4 Spoon half of the mixture into the holes in the prepared muffin tin. Place a piece of marzipan in the centre of each cup, then spoon in the remaining mixture. Top each muffin with a whole almond. Bake in the preheated oven for 20 minutes, or until well risen, golden and firm.

5 Serve warm or transfer to a wire rack and leave to cool.

★ **Variation**

For Strawberry & Amaretto Marzipan Muffins, add 1 tablespoon of amaretto and 12 chopped strawberries to the muffin mixture.

SOMETHING SPECIAL MUFFINS

MUESLI MUFFINS

Makes: 12

Prep: 20 mins, plus cooling

Cook: 20 mins

Ingredients

140 g/5 oz plain flour

1 tbsp baking powder

280 g/10 oz unsweetened muesli

115 g/4 oz soft light brown sugar

2 eggs

250 ml/9 fl oz buttermilk

6 tbsp sunflower oil, plus extra for greasing

Method

1 Preheat the oven to 200°C/400°F/Gas Mark 6. Grease a 12-cup muffin tin or line with 12 paper cases.

2 Sift together the flour and baking powder into a large bowl. Stir in the muesli and sugar.

3 Place the eggs in a large jug or bowl and beat lightly, then beat in the buttermilk and oil. Make a well in the centre of the dry ingredients and pour in the beaten liquid ingredients. Stir gently until just combined; do not over-mix.

4 Divide the mixture evenly between the holes in the prepared muffin tin. Bake in the preheated oven for about 20 minutes, or until well risen, golden and firm to the touch. Serve warm or transfer to a wire rack and leave to cool.

LOW-FAT BANANA & DATE MUFFINS

Makes: 12

Prep: 20 mins,
plus cooling

Cook: 20-25 mins

Ingredients

oil or melted butter,
for greasing (if using)

215 g/7½ oz plain flour

2 tsp baking powder

¼ tsp salt

½ tsp ground mixed spice

5 tbsp caster sugar

2 egg whites

2 ripe bananas, sliced

75 g/2¾ oz ready-to-eat
dried dates, stoned and
chopped

4 tbsp skimmed milk

5 tbsp maple syrup

Method

1 Preheat the oven to 200°C/400°F/Gas Mark 6.
Grease a 12-cup muffin tin or line with 12
paper cases.

2 Sift together the flour, baking powder, salt and
mixed spice into a large bowl. Add the sugar
and mix together.

3 In a separate large bowl, whisk the egg whites.
Mash the bananas in another bowl, then add
them to the egg whites. Add the dates, then
pour in the milk and maple syrup and stir
together gently to mix. Make a well in the centre
of the dry ingredients and pour in the liquid
ingredients. Stir gently until just combined; do not
over-mix.

4 Divide the mixture evenly between the holes in
the prepared muffin tin. Bake in the preheated
oven for 20–25 minutes, or until well risen, golden
and firm to the touch.

5 Serve warm or transfer to a wire rack and leave
to cool.

SUGAR-FREE CHOCOLATE & BLUEBERRY MUFFINS

Makes: 12

Prep: 20 mins, plus cooling

Cook: 20 mins

Ingredients

225 g/8 oz plain flour

1 tbsp baking powder

1 tbsp cocoa powder

½ tsp ground mixed spice

2 eggs

4 tbsp vegetable oil, plus extra for greasing

175 ml/6 fl oz orange juice

grated rind of ½ orange

100 g/3½ oz fresh blueberries

Method

1 Preheat the oven to 200°C/400°F/Gas Mark 6. Grease a 12-cup muffin tin or line with 12 paper cases. Sift together the flour, baking powder, cocoa powder and mixed spice into a large bowl.

2 Lightly beat the eggs with the oil in a large jug. Pour in the orange juice, then add the orange rind and blueberries, and gently stir together to mix. Make a well in the centre of the dry ingredients and pour in the beaten liquid ingredients. Gently stir until just combined; do not over-mix.

3 Divide the mixture evenly between the holes in the prepared muffin tin. Bake in the preheated oven for 20 minutes, or until well risen and firm to the touch.

4 Serve warm or transfer to a wire rack and leave to cool.

NECTARINE & BANANA MUFFINS

Makes: 12

Prep: 25 mins, plus cooling

Cook: 20 mins

Ingredients

250 g/9 oz plain flour

1 tsp bicarbonate of soda

¼ tsp salt

¼ tsp ground allspice

100 g/3½ oz caster sugar

55 g/2 oz almonds, chopped

175 g/6 oz ripe nectarine, peeled, stoned and chopped

1 ripe banana, sliced

2 large eggs

75 ml/2½ fl oz sunflower or groundnut oil, plus extra for greasing

75 ml/2½ fl oz thick natural or banana-flavoured yogurt

1 tsp almond extract

Method

1 Preheat the oven to 200°C/400°F/Gas Mark 6. Grease a 12-cup muffin tin or line with 12 paper cases. Sift together the flour, bicarbonate of soda, salt and allspice into a large bowl. Stir in the sugar and almonds.

2 In a separate large bowl, mash the nectarine and banana, then beat in the eggs, oil, yogurt and almond extract. Make a well in the centre of the dry ingredients and pour in the beaten liquid ingredients. Stir gently until just combined; do not over-mix.

3 Divide the mixture evenly between the holes in the prepared muffin tin. Bake in the preheated oven for 20 minutes, or until well risen, golden and firm to the touch.

4 Serve warm or transfer to a wire rack and leave to cool.

GLUTEN-FREE HONEY & LEMON MUFFINS

Makes: 12

Prep: 20 mins, plus cooling

Cook: 18–20 mins

Ingredients

125 g/4½ oz gluten-free plain flour

120 g/4¼ oz gluten-free polenta

55 g/2 oz caster sugar

2 tsp gluten-free baking powder

¼ tsp xanthan gum

1 egg

juice and rind of ½ lemon

50 ml/2 fl oz vegetable oil, plus extra for greasing

225 ml/8 fl oz milk

2 tbsp honey

1 tbsp glycerine

Method

1 Preheat the oven to 180°C/350°F/Gas Mark 4. Grease a 12-cup muffin tin or line with 12 paper cases.

2 Place the flour, polenta, sugar, baking powder and xanthan gum into a large bowl and mix together well.

3 Lightly beat the egg with the lemon juice and rind, oil, milk, honey and glycerine in a large jug. Make a well in the centre of the dry ingredients and pour in the beaten liquid ingredients. Gently stir until just combined; do not over-mix.

4 Divide the mixture evenly between the holes in the prepared muffin tin. Bake in the preheated oven for 18–20 minutes, or until well risen, golden and firm to the touch. Serve warm or transfer to a wire rack and leave to cool.

BIRTHDAY MUFFINS

Makes: 12

Prep: 30 mins, plus cooling

Cook: 25 mins

Ingredients

280 g / 10 oz plain flour

1 tbsp baking powder

pinch of salt

115 g / 4 oz caster sugar

2 eggs

250 ml / 9 fl oz milk

85 g / 3 oz butter, melted, plus extra for greasing

finely grated rind of 1 lemon

12 birthday candles and candleholders, to decorate

Frosting

85 g / 3 oz butter

175 g / 6 oz icing sugar

Method

1 Preheat the oven to 200°C/400°F/Gas Mark 6. Grease a 12-cup muffin tin or line with 12 paper cases. Sift together the flour, baking powder and salt into a large bowl. Stir in the caster sugar.

2 Lightly beat the eggs in a large jug, then beat in the milk, melted butter and lemon rind. Make a well in the centre of the dry ingredients and pour in the beaten liquid ingredients. Stir gently until just combined; do not over-mix.

3 Divide the mixture evenly between the holes in the prepared muffin tin. Bake in the preheated oven for about 20 minutes, or until well risen, golden and firm to the touch.

4 Transfer to a wire rack and leave to cool.

5 To make the frosting, put the butter in a large bowl and beat until fluffy. Sift in the icing sugar and beat together until smooth and creamy. Spread each muffin with a little of the frosting, then place a candleholder and candle on top.

CHOCOLATE MARSHMALLOW MUFFINS

Makes: 12

Prep: 20 mins,
plus cooling

Cook: 20 mins

Ingredients

100 g/3½ oz white mini marshmallows

225 g/8 oz plain flour

55 g/2 oz cocoa powder

1 tbsp baking powder

pinch of salt

115 g/4 oz soft light brown sugar

2 eggs

250 ml/9 fl oz milk

6 tbsp sunflower oil or 85 g/3 oz butter, melted, plus extra for greasing

Method

1 Preheat the oven to 200°C/400°F/Gas Mark 6. Grease a 12-cup muffin tin or line with 12 paper cases. Using scissors, cut the marshmallows in half.

2 Sift together the flour, cocoa powder, baking powder and salt into a large bowl. Stir in the sugar and marshmallows.

3 Lightly beat the eggs in a large jug, then beat in the milk and oil. Make a well in the centre of the dry ingredients and pour in the beaten liquid ingredients. Stir gently until just combined; do not over-mix.

4 Divide the mixture evenly between the holes in the prepared muffin tin. Bake in the preheated oven for about 20 minutes, or until well risen and firm to the touch.

5 Serve warm or transfer to a wire rack and leave to cool.

SOMETHING SPECIAL MUFFINS

MALTED CHOCOLATE MUFFINS

Makes: 12

Prep: 30 mins,
plus cooling

Cook: 30 mins

Ingredients

150 g/5½ oz malted
chocolate balls

225 g/8 oz plain flour

55 g/2 oz cocoa powder

1 tbsp baking powder

pinch of salt

115 g/4 oz soft light
brown sugar

2 eggs

250 ml/9 fl oz buttermilk

85 g/3 oz butter, melted,
plus extra for greasing

Frosting

55 g/2 oz plain chocolate,
broken into pieces

115 g/4 oz butter, softened

225 g/8 oz icing sugar

Method

1 Preheat the oven to 200°C/400°F/Gas Mark 6.
Grease a 12-cup muffin tin or line with 12
paper cases. Roughly crush the chocolate
balls, reserving 12 whole ones to decorate.

2 Sift together the flour, cocoa powder, baking
powder and salt into a large bowl. Stir in the
brown sugar and the crushed chocolate balls.

3 Lightly beat the eggs in a large jug, then beat in
the buttermilk and melted butter. Make a well
in the centre of the dry ingredients and pour in
the beaten liquid ingredients. Stir gently until just
combined; do not over-mix.

4 Divide the mixture evenly between the holes in
the prepared muffin tin. Bake in the preheated
oven for about 20 minutes, or until well risen
and firm.

5 Transfer to a wire rack and leave to cool.

6 To make the frosting, melt the chocolate in
a heatproof bowl set over a pan of gently
simmering water. Remove from the heat. Put
the butter in a large bowl and beat until fluffy.
Sift in the icing sugar and beat together until
smooth and creamy. Add the melted chocolate
and beat together until well mixed. Spread the
frosting on top of the muffins and decorate each
with one of the reserved chocolate balls.

SOMETHING SPECIAL MUFFINS

POLENTA & CHILLI MUFFINS

Makes: 10   **Prep: 20 mins**   **Cook: 25 mins**

Ingredients

175 g/6 oz self-raising flour

175 g/6 oz polenta

85 g/3 oz caster sugar

2 tsp baking powder

55 g/2 oz hard cheese, finely grated

1 tbsp roughly chopped fresh rosemary

2–3 tsp chilli paste or purée

250 ml/9 fl oz milk

85 g/3 oz butter, melted, plus extra for greasing

1 large egg

1 tsp English mustard

Method

1 Preheat the oven to 200°C/400°F/Gas Mark 6. Grease a 10-cup muffin tin or line with 10 paper cases.

2 Mix the flour, polenta, sugar and baking powder together and sift into a large bowl. Stir in the cheese, rosemary and chilli.

3 Whisk the milk, butter, egg and mustard together in a jug. Pour the mixture over the dry ingredients. Stir until just combined. Don't over-mix and don't worry if there are still some small lumps remaining.

4 Divide the mixture evenly between the holes in the prepared muffin tin. Bake in the preheated oven for 20 minutes, or until well risen, golden and firm to the touch. Serve the muffins warm.

HERB & SMOKED CHEESE MUFFINS

Makes: 12

Prep: 20 mins, plus cooling

Cook: 25 mins

Ingredients

280 g/10 oz plain flour

2 tsp baking powder

½ tsp bicarbonate of soda

25 g/1 oz smoked hard cheese, grated

50 g/1¾ oz fresh parsley, finely chopped

1 egg

300 ml/10 fl oz thick natural yogurt

55 g/2 oz butter, melted, plus extra for greasing

Method

1 Preheat the oven to 200°C/400°F/Gas Mark 6. Grease a 12-cup muffin tin or line with 12 paper cases.

2 Sift together the flour, baking powder and bicarbonate of soda into a large bowl. Stir in the cheese and parsley.

3 Lightly beat the egg in a large jug, then beat in the yogurt and melted butter. Make a well in the centre of the dry ingredients and pour in the beaten liquid ingredients. Stir gently until just combined; do not over-mix.

4 Divide the mixture evenly between the holes in the prepared muffin tin. Bake in the preheated oven for 20 minutes, or until well risen, golden and firm to the touch.

5 Serve warm or transfer to a wire rack and leave to cool.

MOZZARELLA & ROAST PEPPER MUFFINS

Makes: 10

Prep: 25 mins, plus cooling

Cook: 20–25 mins

Ingredients

250 g/9 oz plain flour

2 tsp baking powder

1 tsp bicarbonate of soda

1½ tsp dried oregano

1 tsp salt

½ tsp pepper

25 g/1 oz freshly grated Parmesan cheese

2 eggs

200 ml/7 fl oz buttermilk

3 tbsp light olive oil, plus extra for greasing

115 g/4 oz mozzarella cheese, diced

85 g/3 oz roasted red peppers in brine or oil, drained and cut into strips

Method

1 Preheat the oven to 200°C/400°F/Gas Mark 6. Grease a 10-cup muffin tin or line with 10 paper cases. Sift together the flour, baking powder and bicarbonate of soda into a large bowl. Stir in the oregano, salt, pepper and Parmesan cheese.

2 Lightly beat the eggs in a jug, then beat in the buttermilk and oil. Make a well in the centre of the dry ingredients and pour in the beaten liquid ingredients. Stir gently until just combined; do not over-mix. Gently fold in nearly all of the mozzarella cheese and sliced peppers.

3 Divide the mixture evenly between the holes in the prepared muffin tin. Top with the remaining mozzarella cheese and peppers. Bake in the preheated oven for 20–25 minutes, or until well risen, golden and firm to the touch.

4 Serve warm or transfer to a wire rack and leave to cool.

★ Variation

These muffins would also taste great with goat's cheese instead of the mozzarella.

INDEX

INDEX

This edition published by Parragon Books Ltd in 2014
LOVE FOOD is an imprint of Parragon Books Ltd

Parragon Books Ltd
Chartist House
15–17 Trim Street
Bath BA1 1HA, UK
www.parragon.com/lovefood

Copyright © Parragon Books Ltd 2014

LOVE FOOD and the accompanying heart device is a registered
trademark of Parragon Books Ltd in Australia, the UK, USA, India and the
EU.

ISBN 978-1-4723-5998-8
Printed in China

Cover photography by Ian Garlick
Introduction by Anne Sheasby

Notes for the Reader
This book uses both metric and imperial measurements. Follow the
same units of measurement throughout; do not mix metric and imperial.
All spoon measurements are level: teaspoons are assumed to be 5 ml,
and tablespoons are assumed to be 15 ml. Unless otherwise stated, milk
is assumed to be full fat, eggs and individual vegetables are medium,
and pepper is freshly ground black pepper. Unless otherwise stated, all
root vegetables should be peeled prior to using.

Garnishes, decorations and serving suggestions are all optional and
not necessarily included in the recipe ingredients or method. The
times given are an approximate guide only. Preparation times differ
according to the techniques used by different people and the cooking
times may also vary from those given. Optional ingredients, variations or
serving suggestions have not been included in the time calculations.